WOMEN
— OF —
THE NEW
TESTAMENT

Strong Was Her Faith

J. ELLSWORTH KALAS

Abingdon Press
NASHVILLE

STRONG WAS HER FAITH
WOMEN OF THE NEW TESTAMENT

Library of Congress Cataloging-in-Publication Data

Kalas, J. Ellsworth, 1923-
    Strong was her faith : women of the New Testament / J. Ellsworth Kalas.
        p.   cm.
    (binding: adhesive, perfect : alk. paper)
    1. Women in the Bible.   I. Title.

BS2445.K35 2007
225.9'22082—dc22

ISBN-13: 978-1-4267-4465-5

2006030279

12 13 14 15 16 17 18 19 20 21—10 9 8 7 6 5 4 3 2 1
MANUFACTURED IN THE UNITED STATES OF AMERICA

A long generation ago most churches had some faithful worker who was called "the church secretary." In more recent years we have developed a variety of titles that we hope might describe these persons more adequately. Whatever the name, their role is often priceless. I'm confident that most readers of this book, whether clergy or laity, will immediately identify such an individual from their experience.

I want to dedicate this book to three such persons who blessed my pastoral ministry over the years:

J. Emory Temple
Beverley Reed
Bobbie Buchs

Other Titles by J. Ellsworth Kalas

Contents

CONTENTS

Foreword

Several years ago, soon after the publishing of my book *The Thirteen Apostles,* I was speaking at a church in the Greater Washington, D.C., area. The director of adult education said during a coffee hour, "Now you should write a book about the *women* in the New Testament." I agreed that such a book should be written but protested that perhaps the author should not be a man. She insisted kindly that I could do the job fairly and well, so I have ever since kept her counsel in the back of my mind and soul. This book is the result.

You might rightly ask about some of the women I have included, since in some instances the biblical references are few and brief. I can only counter that the same is true of such apostles as Simon the Zealot, James the Less, and Thaddeus. Where possible I have supplemented the biblical material with some of the traditions and legends that have grown around these persons, making clear that such material is treated for what it is and not as historical data. In every instance, of course, I have tried to find the "plot line" in the person's story—the passing incident or the brief words that reveal character and that provide a kind of holy trajectory.

I should tell you that I found it difficult to narrow my list to a desired number. I wish I could have included Phoebe, described by Paul as "a benefactor of many" (Romans 16:2), and the mother of Rufus, to whom Paul affectionately referred as "a mother to me also" (Romans 16:13). And how about the "four unmarried daughters" of Philip, "who had the gift of prophecy" (Acts 21:9)? Or that wonderfully insistent mother who worked so earnestly on behalf of her sons, James and John (Matthew 20:20-28)? I'm almost certain some of you will write to object to some of my choices, while offering recommendations of your own. Thus I make this early appeal for clemency.

I want to pay special thanks to one of my students, Shannon Sumrall. I enlisted her help in several instances of background research. She not only did this research with admirable skill but also added insights of her own several times. In those two or three instances where I mention an insight from an unnamed student or friend, you can insert Shannon's name.

—*J. Ellsworth Kalas*

CHAPTER ONE

Elizabeth:
A Friend in Need

Scripture Reading: Luke 1:39-45

Next to Mary, the Mother of Jesus, Elizabeth was the first woman to recognize and serve our Lord, and she began doing so before he was even born.

Many of the most notable Christians come to faith by dramatically negative paths: Paul as the premier persecutor of Christians; Augustine as a libertine; C. S. Lewis and many others as, at first, atheists. Elizabeth came by a path of virtue. From all we can know, she was an exemplary human being.

Her genealogy gave her a head start toward virtue. She came, not simply from good stock, but from great, enviable stock. When Luke introduces her to his readers in an early paragraph of his Gospel, he gives her ancestry before mentioning her name: After noting that there is a priest named Zechariah, Luke continues, "His wife was a descendant of Aaron, and her name was Elizabeth" (Luke 1:5). This was to say not only that she "came over on the *Mayflower*," so to speak, but also that she traveled in a stateroom. Aaron was Moses' brother and Israel's first high priest. He made some egregious mistakes, but he was in a class altogether to himself. If Elizabeth had been a man, she would have been a priest by right of descent and potentially perhaps even a high priest.

Then she married well. Staying not only within the levitical clan, she married someone who was also a descendant of Aaron, "a priest named Zechariah, who belonged to the priestly order of Abijah" (Luke 1:5). This, as the saying goes, was a union made in heaven.

But the fairy-tale quality of their marriage stumbled there. Luke puts it without embellishment: "But they had no children" (Luke 1:7). He could have gone on to explain that in their time and place, for a marriage to be childless was both a tragedy and an embarrassment. Jewish rabbis said that seven people were excommunicated from God, and first on the list was "a Jew who has no wife, or a Jew who has a wife and who has no child."[1] That is, to be childless was far

2

more than disappointment and personal heartbreak. There were theological implications; it was as if God had not really approved of the marriage.

But with all of this, Luke nevertheless tells us, "Both of them were righteous before God, living blamelessly according to all the commandments and regulations of the Lord" (Luke 1:6). *"Righteous, blameless"*—I'm struck by the fact that the book of Genesis uses the same words to describe Noah. I doubt that the times were quite as bad in Elizabeth's era as in Noah's, when "every inclination of the thoughts of [human] hearts was only evil continually" (Genesis 6:5), but the times were bad enough. There was peace, but it was the enforced peace of a powerful Roman military; slavery was a way of life and commerce; and moral corruption not only abounded, it was sanctioned in high places. At such a time, our planet needed some sort of redemptive visitation. These visits are not often by angels; mostly God intervenes in our planet through human beings—many kinds of humans, but especially when they are available, "righteous, blameless" humans. Elizabeth and Zechariah were such.

But who knew about this couple? True, Zechariah was a member of a rather large, if exclusive, company of priests, but they were important only to the somewhat despised sect of the Jewish people. For most of the then known world, what happened in a Jewish temple mattered little. If you were an intellectual, you cared about Athens or Alexandria; and if you wanted to get into real power, the world of politics, there

3

was Rome. Only God and a few saintly souls cared about what was happening in Jerusalem. And if I know anything about human nature, some in Jerusalem weren't necessarily impressed by Zechariah and Elizabeth. After all, they couldn't have children, so there could always be gossip about what was wrong in their lives—why were they not favored by God? I venture there were women at the well in Zechariah and Elizabeth's village who said, "Elizabeth may have good ancestors, but I have babies."

Then special good fortune came Zechariah's way. It is estimated that at that time there were as many as twenty thousand priests, so the company was broken into sections to serve at particular seasons; and from those sections a priest was chosen by lot to offer a morning or evening sacrifice for the entire nation. A priest might go all his life without this holy chance. Now, the opportunity fell on Zechariah. As he ministered in this singular setting, an angel of the Lord appeared to him, to tell him that he and Elizabeth would have a son, whom they should call John. We will later know him as John the Baptist. But wonderful as this promise was, it was not simply a private blessing. It was appropriate that Zechariah should receive this revelation while he was in prayer for the spiritual welfare of his nation, because this child, the angel said, would be "great in the sight of the Lord," and would "turn many of the people of Israel to the Lord their God" (Luke 1:15-16).

So Elizabeth did, indeed, conceive. When she was in the

sixth month of her pregnancy (see Luke 1:26), something still more momentous happened. Gabriel, the same angel who had visited Zechariah, now came to a virgin named Mary, who was "engaged to a man whose name was Joseph," to tell her that she was to have a child by the Holy Spirit, who would "be called Son of God" (Luke 1:26-35).

Twenty centuries later, you and I read this story with the knowledge that millions now refer to this peasant girl as "the blessed Virgin Mary," but at that time she was more particularly the frightened Virgin Mary. Even after she was assured that she was God's "favored one," and that what was happening in her life was by God's action, she had to cope with the hard facts of a fiancé who almost surely would not understand, a family that would fear humiliation and censure, and a little town that might never stop gossiping. Gabriel might have been right when he announced that "nothing will be impossible with God" (Luke 1:37), but God was in heaven, and Mary had to live in her village.

So Mary needed a friend, and this is where Elizabeth—a woman of many virtues—demonstrated her most notable greatness: She was Mary's friend. We sometimes speak of a person being a "soul friend"; the title could have been born with Elizabeth. As Luke tells the story, it appears that after Mary's visit from Gabriel she wasted no time in seeking out Elizabeth. As the writer puts it, "In those days Mary set out and went with haste to a Judean town in the hill country" (Luke 1:39). When she entered the house and called out her greeting to Elizabeth (was it the Aramaic equivalent of the "Yoo-hoo!" women neighbors used in my boyhood?), "the child leaped in [Elizabeth's] womb" (Luke 1:41).

I've already said that Elizabeth was a righteous woman. At this moment we know how righteous she was. "And Elizabeth was filled with the Holy Spirit and exclaimed [to Mary] with a loud cry, 'Blessed are you among women, and blessed is the fruit of your womb. And why has this happened to me, that the mother of my Lord comes to me?'" (Luke 1:41-43, adapted). I am impressed that Elizabeth was so sensitive to the Holy Spirit that she was open to the revelation of what God was doing in the life of her young relative, Mary. I admit that I am very cautious when people speak too easily of God's voice and God's leading in their lives because I know how human all of us are, and therefore how susceptible we are to attributing to God what may be only our own emotional fervor. But I believe that God's Spirit is at work in our world, and I suspect we might hear from God more often if we were more open to the divine voice. As far as we know, without having received any information from Mary, Elizabeth knew that Mary was carrying a unique child in her womb.

Let me interrupt the holy, ecstatic quality of this moment to speak to a very human element in the story. Elizabeth is six months pregnant with a baby she has prayed for since the day she and Zechariah first were pledged to one another. Her baby is a miracle baby. If Elizabeth responds to life the way most of us do, her natural focus at this moment is not on her young relative and that relative's baby, but on her own exciting prospects. We will understand if Elizabeth begins telling Mary about her child-to-be, this miracle son with prophetic credentials: "Even before his birth he will be filled with the Holy Spirit. He will turn many of the people of Israel to the Lord their God" (Luke 1:15-16). Elizabeth has been bursting with this excitement for six months and more, and probably has had few people, if any, with whom she could share it. Now her young relative is here, a person sensitive enough to appreciate Elizabeth's story.

But instead of telling her story, Elizabeth turns all her attention on Mary: "Blessed are you among women, and blessed is the fruit of your womb. And why has this happened to me, that the mother of my Lord comes to me? For as soon as I heard the sound of your greeting, the child in my womb leaped for joy" (Luke 1:42-44). There would come a time in Jesus' ministry when he would challenge potential followers, "Whoever comes to me and does not hate father and mother, wife and children, brothers and sisters, yes, and even life itself, cannot be my disciple" (Luke 14:26). This was the dramatic Middle Eastern way of saying that if one were to follow Jesus, one must prize him above all other human relationships. I submit that Elizabeth was the first to commit such allegiance to our Lord. At a time when no human relationship mattered more to her than that of the son soon to be born to her, Elizabeth chose to rejoice in

Mary's son. So it was that this woman made an utterly unselfish step of apostolic discipleship. She had greeted Mary as "the mother of my Lord." In doing so, she was the first to hail Jesus as Lord. And in her act of putting aside her own natural family love to honor Mary's son, she proved that she meant it when she referred to Mary's son as "my Lord."

Let me add another word. Some thirty years later Elizabeth's son, John the Baptist, would be perhaps the most notable religious personality in Israel, with thousands flocking from all over Israel to visit John in the wilderness, many of them seeking baptism. The crowds would include numbers of religious leaders. At this pinnacle of public acclaim, John one day pointed to Jesus and said to some of his followers, "Look, here is the Lamb of God!" (John 1:36). Immediately the two men to whom John was speaking left him to follow Jesus. Before long, most of the crowds had forsaken John. When someone reported to John that the crowds were now going after Jesus, John replied in what seems an almost matter-of-fact way that this was the way it was supposed to be. "He must increase," John said, "but I must decrease" (John 3:30). I dare to suggest that John caught this spirit of self-abnegation from his mother while he was still in her womb.

Think of Elizabeth as a woman with an uncommon gift for friendship. In truth, it was a divinely ordained gift. She spoke her loyalty to her cousin Mary as she was "filled with the Holy Spirit" (Luke 1:41). Theologians have written thou-

8

sands of pages about what it means to be filled with the Holy
Spirit. I don't mean to oversimplify, but I'm very sure
Elizabeth has given us an example that is worth a book or
two. When one is filled with God's Spirit, one enters a sacred
chamber of unselfishness. Elizabeth cared so much for Mary
that she could forget her own admirable excitements; she
believed so deeply in what the Holy Spirit was saying to her
about Mary's son that she could declare him as Lord even
before his birth, and she could subjugate her profound love
for her own soon-to-be-born son in order to exalt Mary's
son. This, surely, is the Holy Spirit in action. Elizabeth is
speaking the language of a sanctified life, a life wholly given
to God's purposes.

Mary needed just such a friend. It is one thing to experience God deeply in the private place of prayer; it is quite
another to step out into the cold reality of an ordinary day.
An angel had spoken to Mary, but then the angel disap-
peared. Mary needed someone who would be there tomorrow. The angelic visit was a brief ecstasy, but ecstasy is a kind
of meringue on the daily pie of life; it's beautiful and gentle
to the tongue, but the level of nourishment is low. Mary
needed a friend.

And she needed a spiritual friend. I have been blessed by
so many wonderful friends in my lifetime; I'm not being
humble when I say that I've had far more friends than I could
ever deserve. I've learned that friends come in a variety of
styles, and I'm grateful for all of them: the friends who are

great with a glass of iced tea, those with whom it is easy to laugh, and those who provide intellectually stimulating conversation. But there is nothing quite like the friend who has such a close relationship to God that in that person's presence you feel closer to God.

I remember what Mae A. Blackburn meant to my mother. She was a truly godly woman; not in a painfully pious fashion but quite naturally, because faith had become her native air. When my mother was deep-down lonely—something that as a boy I did not understand but could feel—she went to see Mrs. Blackburn. When the Blackburns moved a thousand miles away, Mother waited for her letters the way the people at Philippi waited for an epistle from Paul. When Mother needed prayer, she turned first to Mae Blackburn.

There is nothing quite like a friend who, when he or she says, "I will pray for you," you already begin to feel the tide of hell retreating. Others may listen kindly, some may offer lovely platitudes, but the spiritual friend transfuses strength. As you leave the spiritual friend's presence, you feel ready for the worst that life can bring your way.

This quality comes to those persons who, like Elizabeth, seek to be righteous and blameless before God; and who, like Elizabeth, are filled with the Holy Spirit; and who, like Elizabeth, demonstrate the Spirit's presence by the absolute unselfishness with which they give themselves to others.

Mary needed such a friend. She was embarking upon a journey no other woman before or since has known. She was to become the unique vessel for God's visit to our planet. Her path was set with peril on every side. The pious would say that she needed God; but in truth, what she needed was God visiting her in the magnificently human fashion of a friend. I can't imagine what might have happened to the sacred story if there hadn't been an Elizabeth.

That's why I place Elizabeth first in this story of the women who were crucial in the life and ministry of our Lord, not only because she comes so early in the story but also because I can't imagine what would have happened to the story without her. No wonder, then, that she has a particular quality of apostolic radiance.

CHAPTER TWO

Anna: She Knew How to Wait

Scripture Reading: Luke 2:36-38

I am about to enshrine as a virtue a quality that is very low on the popularity polls. Some would call it patience; I will resort to a euphemism, hoping thus to make it more palatable, but I know I can't fool you for long. I call it "knowing how to wait." We want our children to know how to wait (if they don't, how can we get done the things we just have to

13

do?), but we don't give them much of an example. Nor does our daily culture. In this world where people honk at the car in front of them even before the light changes, and in which a slowdown in the computer is an Armageddon crisis, who wants to learn lessons from someone who knew how to wait? Or who finds virtue in such a person?

God does. That's why Anna is so significant. Anna knew how to wait; and that's why as a woman whose credentials might seem to fit on a pinhead, she has found an esteemed place in the sacred story. She wrote no books, performed no concerts, was elected to no office, but the church knows her as a saint. Of course, waiting is a prime character test for saints. Mind you, I don't think many saints begin with a gift for waiting; from what I've read, many saints begin their pilgrimage in a hurry, and they're often the kind of people who frequently fret along the way. But long before they're ready for canonizing, they became expert waiters.

But back to Anna. She is the third woman to come by name in Jesus' story, after Mary and Elizabeth. Her entrance is so unlikely that she should be an encouragement to any of us who feel we are unlikely to be major contributors to the eternal story. She seems, in fact, to back in to the story. Luke has just recounted the moving story of Simeon, whom God had told that he would not die until he had seen the Messiah (see Luke 2:25-35), and Luke continues, "There was also a prophet, Anna" (Luke 2:36). You're familiar with the "also" feeling; you see it often in newspaper stories, as a concluding paragraph: "*Also* present were..."

14

Nor does the specific identification help much. We are told the name of Anna's father, Phanuel, though we know nothing more about him, and that she was from the tribe of Asher. Asher was one of the least known of Jacob's sons. The Asher tribe was fortunate in having some of the mineral-rich land, but this tribe gets few lines in the nation's story. Nevertheless, there's something significant here. Asher was one of the ten northern tribes that were taken captive by Assyria in 722 B.C. and eventually lost to us through inter-marriage with other peoples of the Middle East. But a small number of people from the various northern tribes stayed with the southern nation that came to be known as Judah, usually because they wanted to be near Jerusalem so they could participate in the temple worship and in the holy feast days. I think it can rightly be said that anyone from a north-ern tribe who still resided in first-century Palestine was descended from someone who had originally chosen that ter-ritory for religious reasons. Which is to say, Anna had a good faith lineage.

She was a woman "of great age." Anna had been married only seven years when she was widowed. She had never remarried. Now she was eighty-four years old. It seems cer-tain that she had no children. Life, as the saying goes, had not treated her kindly. Someone has said that trouble can make a person bitter or better. It's clear that loss and sorrow and deprivation made Anna better.

This brings us to a phrase, you may have noticed, that I

skipped over without comment: Anna was "a prophet." At the very least, this means that Anna was especially gifted by God. It was a gift that was marked, not by a wall diploma, but by common recognition of her peers. No recognition is more significant than this, and none harder to come by. Women have found this to be true throughout so much of history, particularly in many parts of the first-century world. There were occasional women prophets—one thinks immediately of Deborah (Judges 4) and Huldah (2 Kings 22) in the Old Testament—but they were a rare body, for sure. I repeat, their gift had to make room for them, because the culture didn't encourage the idea of a woman assuming such a position of spiritual leadership. To be more emphatic, a woman couldn't assume such a role; it had to come to her by way of those who recognized an extraordinary talent and weren't afraid to say so.

Luke continues that Anna "never left the temple but worshiped there with fasting and prayer night and day" (Luke 2:37). I'm quite sure that in some sense this statement is metaphorical, because it would have been physically impossible to manage all the functions of life within the temple. Even so, Luke is making clear that for Anna the temple was her whole life. It wasn't simply a place where she came for occasions of worship or at set hours of the day. It was where, whatever the day or whatever the hour, you would be most likely to find Anna. We preachers sometimes say of certain devoted people, "They're in church whenever the church doors are open." That was Anna's style, only more so.

But how then did she make a living? Even someone on the way to sainthood has to eat. It is possible, of course, that Anna's husband had left her some means of sustenance, but I think it's quite unlikely there was enough to keep her for half a century or more. Consider that she is called "a prophet." When we think of biblical prophets, we think of their public declarations. But they weren't pastors for whom offerings were received, and only a few of them were in the priestly line, where their work was supported by the community structure. The Scriptures suggest, however, that the prophets were also spiritual advisors to the people—in some cases, even to kings. In a sense, they were consultants—holy consultants, if you will. A friend who has been a financial consultant tells me that it's a good living if you have enough clients. Anna probably had an irregular following of clients, and I'm quite sure they didn't reward her as generously as people reward financial consultants today. At best, her income had to have been an uncertain affair.

Still another word should be said about Anna as prophet. We often speak of John the Baptist as the first prophet after a lapse of several centuries between the Old Testament and the New. As a matter of fact, Anna is the first person named a prophet in the New Testament. She was a generation ahead of John; but in a quiet way she had the same calling, to prepare the way for the Messiah. John did so before growing crowds, and eventually in the midst of fatal controversy, while Anna ministered in a quiet way—an unassuming posture that must have characterized all her life.

How is it that she recognized Jesus so quickly? We can understand how Simeon might do so, since he had been promised he wouldn't die until he saw the Messiah; thus he was constantly on the watch. We have no evidence that Anna worked with such an assurance. We don't even know that she was awaiting the Messiah—not any more than any earnest and pious Jew of her time. How is it, then, that she knew this baby when he was brought for the temple rites? Over her long life no doubt she had seen literally thousands of infants brought to the temple; how did she know Jesus when Joseph and Mary brought him there?

Well, that's one of the benefits that come from knowing how to wait. Because, for a Christian, knowing how to wait isn't simply a matter of sitting around, struggling with impatience. A key element in godly waiting is the mood in which one does the waiting. Anna was someone who was constantly in "fasting and prayer." For her, waiting was a holy enterprise, and it made her sensitive to eternity and to the purposes of God that most of us mortals rarely know. In a way, it's very simple. Those of us who live by the business news come to sense the economic tides; those who consume fashion publications know what "look" will be "in" this fall; those who love the sports pages and the sports channels can tell you the odds on who will win what trophy. Just so, those who absorb themselves with eternity get a feeling for eternity's movements in time. A friend of mine suggests that as a result of the life she had been living, Anna was so in tune with God that when she saw Mary and Joseph with their baby, "there wasn't a moment of hesitation. 'There he is!' "

Anna couldn't keep this ecstatic moment to herself. She "began to praise God and to speak about the child to all who were looking for the redemption of Jerusalem" (Luke 2:38). And because Anna was a prophet, with years of what our world would call "brand-name recognition" but what her generation knew as integrity and righteousness, what she said carried great weight. Nevertheless, it appears that she chose where she would witness. Exuberant as she may have been, she didn't simply broadcast the news; she delivered it "to all who were looking for the redemption of Jerusalem" (Luke 2:38).

I think this indicates that she was part of a group of devout Jews in Jerusalem who had been praying for the coming of the Messiah. She obviously knew who they were, and she was herself one of them. No doubt they had encouraged one another. Perhaps Anna herself might have lost heart at times if she had not been sustained by these fellow waiters. She may have been the strongest of the lot and the most saintly, but at times even the most saintly have survived only because much weaker people have come alongside with a good word.

The Bible tells us nothing more about Anna. Tradition and legends have added to her story, however. Early in church history her name was linked with Judith from the Apocrypha, as a model for widowhood and to illustrate

19

sermons based on the passage in Paul's First Letter to Timothy regarding widows in the church (see 1 Timothy 5:3-16). Young widows in the early centuries of our era faced enormous problems, because there was virtually no honorable way for them to earn a living. A preacher or teacher who was trying to encourage such persons was glad to point to Anna as a noble example. If Anna, widowed after only seven years of marriage, could not only survive but also become a prophet and an example and the second witness to the newborn Christ Child, young widows in the church could take heart.

In time a particular tradition grew in the Catholic Church: that Anna became tutor and spiritual guide to Mary the mother of Jesus. It's a lovely thought, even if hard to prove. One enjoys imagining an immediate sense of closeness between the aged widow and the teenaged mother. It isn't an uncommon kind of story, so it's easy to give credence to the tradition. One thing is sure: Anna didn't pray as did Simeon that having seen God's purposes brought to pass, she was ready now to die. In the passage recorded in Luke 2:36-38, Anna is eighty-four years old, with no recorded thought of finishing her career. All of us have known grandmothers and great-grandmothers who got a new lease on life at the prospect of helping a young mother. Perhaps Anna had such an experience.

And all the more so because Anna never had any children of her own. Some of the greatest mothers I have ever known were women who never married or had children, but who with singular kindness tended to the children of other people. I have often pondered that three of my earliest-remembered Sunday school teachers were what in those days were called "maiden ladies." They seemed to find time for other people's children. Who knows what basis there is for the Catholic tradition regarding Anna?

But in truth, Anna needs no help from tradition. Her story, succinct as it is in Luke's Gospel, is enough. In a world that was difficult enough for women in general and desperately difficult for single women and widows, Anna not only survived, she overcame. We cannot know whether for some years—still such a young woman—she dreamed of marrying again and of having children. Perhaps she went almost immediately into her unique ministry of prayer and fasting, but perhaps it was only after a titanic inner struggle that she did so.

And as time went by, Anna became a person who *waited*. Believers are great at that, you know. Others may feel that the passing days are without meaning, something to be counted off as painlessly and as quickly as possible. People of faith learn better. We discover that in our waiting we come to know God better; we get the time to think about God as well as ourselves. Ironically, in that process we also come to know ourselves better. Most of us, most of the time, know ourselves only superficially. We need time enough to stand off at a distance from our own souls, to become as objective as possible about ourselves (a huge undertaking!), so that we can see both our baseness and our grandeur. We need this balance in our self-knowing, and that takes time.

But especially, as we wait, we come to understand life. Perhaps this is why the very old and the very young sometimes say things that astonish us for their depth. The very old have more time to themselves (even if sometimes unwillingly), and the very young—provided we don't clutter their lives with too much organized activity and too many adult-made toys—think in unfettered ways. With time we learn that life cannot be neatly compartmentalized, can't always be managed, and can almost never be hurried up. We learn to cooperate with time rather than fight it. And we learn, if we have any measure of faith, that God is wonderfully and mysteriously involved in time.

Having just mentioned faith, let me also say that knowing how to wait is a major factor in faith. Faith and impatience are sworn enemies. To have faith means to be willing to wait. Most great causes have been lost, not for lack of resources or shortage of talent, but for lack of the kind of faith that holds on doggedly, willing to wait and unwilling to hurry off to a new cause.

One of Jesus' loveliest and most penetrating parables is the story of a woman—a widow—who had been treated unjustly. The judge to whom she pleaded her cause had no time for her; Jesus said this judge was a man "who neither feared God nor had respect for people" (Luke 18:2). But the woman was so insistent that the judge, who cared little about justice, gave in to the widow's persistence. This is the way, Jesus said, that we are "to pray always and to not lose heart" (Luke 18:1).

I wonder, I wonder if when Jesus told this story about a widow he may have built his story around a special memory? Surely his mother Mary—probably many times—told him about a woman who was present on the day of his dedication in the temple: a widow, who "never left the temple but worshiped there with fasting and prayer night and day" (Luke 2:37). After all, Jesus shaped all his parables around people and scenes and events that were part of his store of memories; I wonder if Anna was part of that memory store? It could be. Because Anna had a virtue that is hard to come by: She knew how to wait. She knew God well enough to know how to wait. When you're hurried and frazzled tomorrow, think about that.

CHAPTER THREE

Martha,
the Disciplined

Scripture Reading: Luke 10:38-42; John 11:1-27

The several saints all have their times of particular popularity. The very qualities that make a saint especially appealing to one generation can lead to her eclipse in the next. Martha of Bethany is at her best these days, what with the emphasis among theologians on the virtues of hospitality. Who can better exemplify hospitality? Even if she seemed to overdo it or to demonstrate it a bit awkwardly, Martha was committed to hospitality, no doubt about it.

But Martha managed quite well over many centuries before theologians began re-emphasizing the theme of Christian hospitality. Anyone reading this book is almost certain to know someone named Martha, and almost as certain to have an ancestor bearing the name. The popularity of names rises and falls every decade, so I can't guarantee how the name Martha will rank at the time you read this book. But any name that continues over centuries to find its place among the few dozen greatest is a name to be reckoned with, and all the more so when one considers that it has found its place in many tongues.

And what does that have to do with the biblical Martha? Quite simply, that every person who carries the name Martha must look back ultimately to this New Testament woman as the origin for her name. The contemporary Martha may think she is named after an aunt or a grandmother, but trace her name through the family tree, and eventually you will end up somewhere in the Gospels of Luke and John, with Martha.

And yet, when you search out Martha's stories in the New Testament—especially the story best known to the general public—you wonder how it is that Martha became so popular.

The issue begins with Martha's hospitality—her brightest virtue, to which I referred just a moment ago. The Gospel writers indicate that Jesus felt especially comfortable in the home of the siblings Mary, Martha, and Lazarus. Some traditions speculate that Martha was the widow of a wealthy landowner, but the Bible gives us no details about the three except that they maintained a household together and that Jesus was often entertained there. Luke reports on one such occasion. He tells us that Jesus "entered a certain village, where a woman named Martha welcomed him into her home" (Luke 10:38). Luke's language suggests that Martha is the head of the house, the older sister and the one who for some reason controls the family welfare. It may be from this fact that we get the tradition of her being the widow of a wealthy man, because if the property were from her father's family, it would have passed to her brother, Lazarus.

Martha had to be excited about entertaining Jesus. Though his roots were in a back-country village, Nazareth, he had become a well-known teacher, and people had begun to flock to him, sometimes to hear what he taught and probably just as often to see what miracle he might next perform. Like any very hospitable person, Martha wanted everything to be just right for her guests. And as any cook knows, this isn't easy to bring off. So many elements have to come together, not only in their natural compatibility but also in their timing. Let one feature go wrong—a room appointment that is not quite right or a dish that is over- or under-cooked, or over- or under-seasoned—and somehow the whole enterprise collapses.

Martha had dreamed so long of a day like this, a day to entertain the beloved Rabbi, and had planned so exhaustively to make the day just right, and now there was the possibility of its falling apart. Fretting, fumbling, perspiring, she heard laughter from the other room. It was warm laughter, with a kind of frivolity that made one think happy angels were nearby. It was the laughter that did it. It was her sister Mary's laughter, Mary who seemed always to get more attention; Mary the clever, outgoing, carefree one. *Martha* (she said to herself), *Martha carries all of the load and always has. Martha is the big sister who gets blamed when little sister skins her knee, even though I had warned her about the hazards of the hillside; Martha serves as surrogate mother for years (still has to at times!); it was Martha who sometimes had to discipline her siblings and who somehow never did it right, because her discipline was either too severe, too lenient, or too late. Meanwhile, Mary can laugh. Mary has no problems. She doesn't have to manage the limited family exchequer. No wonder she can be so charming, with laughter that lilts as if on angel wings!*

So Martha burst into the adjoining room, where the Rabbi sat talking while Mary sat at his feet, listening so intently. (She has nothing to worry about; she can listen.) Now her concerns burst out: "Lord, do you not care that my sister has left me to do all the work by myself? Tell her then to help me" (Luke 10:40). It is a reasonable request. I recognize the tone of voice. I heard it at times as a boy (the only child still at home), when Mother called from the kitchen at a strategic moment. I have heard the same tone hundreds of times since then in homes where I have been the guest and where some family member was summoned to save the day. I understand the crisis, and my sympathies are with Martha. All the Marthas.

But Jesus doesn't seem to understand. Instead of gently suggesting that Mary do her part, and with equal gentleness calming Martha's concerns, Jesus is strangely unsympathetic. Indeed, he seems to turn the requested reprimand onto the petitioner: "Martha, Martha, you are worried and distracted by many things; there is need of only one thing. Mary has chosen the better part, which will not be taken away from her" (Luke 10:41-42).

And the story ends there. As far as we know, Martha went back to the hot kitchen, where the food was getting out of control, while Mary's laughter continued to trill lightly, ever more happily and exasperatingly. It could be, of course, that Mary suddenly realized that she owed something to her big sister and that the lessons Jesus was teaching were best lived out in helping others, even older siblings. Or it could be that Martha realized what a poor choice she had made, being so "cumbered about much serving," as the King James Version so memorably puts it.

I'll talk more about Mary at another time, but just now I want to concentrate on Martha. I want to say a good word for her. Obviously, for one thing, her intentions were good. She wanted everything to be just right. Having said that, I'll confess, on the one hand, that I've been a guest in some situations where I would have enjoyed myself so much more if the hostess had relaxed enough to let me feel I was a blessing and not a burden. I wonder if, at the moment of Martha's interruption, Jesus felt as if he were a burden? And yet, on the other hand, I've been in situations where I wish Martha had made a prior visit; I would have been more comfortable if she had been there to provide the lovely touches that make a guest feel wanted and honored.

And I praise Martha for her practical good sense and her self-discipline. Some people get to read more, be on the cell phone more frequently, and attend more parties because someone else gets some necessary things done. Martha has a keen eye for her tasks. I suspect she draws up a list in the morning—or more likely, the night before—of what must be done the next day. She does the work of three because she thinks and plans ahead, and disciplines herself to make things happen.

But above all, I want to say that Martha came to know her Lord very well. I like to think that it was because of this experience we've just discussed, but however it was, Martha came to get enough of her sister Mary's insight that she became the well-rounded and fully developed spiritual person she no doubt always wanted to be.

You get the rest of Martha's story in an experience that shook and then transformed the household of Martha, Mary, and Lazarus. John's Gospel records it in detail. Lazarus was ill; we don't know the nature of the illness, but it was serious enough that the sisters sent word to Jesus, believing that if he would come, their brother would be healed. But instead of responding quickly to the appeal, Jesus stayed where he was two days longer, telling his disciples that this would all turn to the glory of God. When at last Jesus told the disciples he was now going to Bethany, he treated the trip rather playfully. "Our friend Lazarus," he said, "has fallen asleep, but I am going there to awaken him." When the disciples indicated that they saw no reason to go if Lazarus were simply sleeping, "Jesus told them plainly, 'Lazarus is dead. For your sake I am glad I was not there, so that you may believe. But let us go to him'" (John 11:11, 14-15).

What follows is one of the crucial chapters in the New Testament story. When they arrived, Lazarus was indeed dead, and had been for four days. Jesus' raising him from the dead was an epochal miracle in its own right, but it also energized the enemies of Jesus to speed up the process of Jesus' arrest, trial, and crucifixion. But I'm passing over this part of the story in order to concentrate on our special interest, Martha.

When Martha learned that Jesus was near, she hurried to meet him; but Mary stayed at home. As I read their two personalities, this isn't the way I expect the story to unfold. Mary is the emotional member of the family, the one who particularly delighted in Jesus' presence; I calculate that she will not only go with Martha to meet Jesus but also will outrun her older sister. Not so. Martha greeted Jesus quite

31

abruptly: "Lord, if you had been here, my brother would not have died" (John 11:21). On the one hand, her greeting was a grand declaration of faith; she had no doubt that whatever her brother's illness, Jesus could have healed him. On the other hand I also hear an accusing quality in Martha's voice, a "you could have done something" tone.

When Jesus answered, "Your brother will rise again," Martha as quickly replied—with the quality of a good lay theologian—"I know that he will rise again in the resurrection on the last day" (John 11:23-24). Then came one of scripture's monumental conversational exchanges. "Jesus said to her, 'I am the resurrection and the life. Those who believe in me, even though they die, will live, and everyone who lives and believes in me will never die. Do you believe this?' She said to him, 'Yes, Lord, I believe that you are the Messiah, the Son of God, the one coming into the world'" (John 11:25-27).

Martha's answer seems to me to be no less powerful than Peter's classic declaration of faith, the one on which Jesus said he would build the church (see Matthew 16:13-18). If Peter's words were an apostolic statement, Martha's surely were not far behind. When Peter spoke his words, Jesus answered, "Flesh and blood has not revealed this to you, but my Father in heaven" (Matthew 16:17). I sense the same kind of Holy Spirit empowering in Martha's statement. Her words seem to be without forethought, as simple as a child's "I love you," and as earthshaking as a ruler's declaration of peace.

They are extraordinary words for a woman we might have passed over as someone more at home cooking and cleaning and providing for the comfort of others. But of course this is dramatically consistent with what our Lord said—"Whoever wishes to be great among you must be your servant" (Matthew 20:26). Martha sought no office of greatness, but she enunciated the faith as well as the master apostle. And more. This woman who might have been written off as rather prosaic, taking life in stride, doing her market and kitchen thing; this woman has as much capacity for emotion as her sister, who is remembered for anointing Jesus with perfume (see John 11:2). All Martha needed was the venue for expression.

I have known several Marthas, and I'm quite sure you have too. I have often heard her described in funeral homes and in social gatherings following a memorial service. "At first we took her for granted," someone says, "until we learned how wise she was." "So much quiet strength." "She never made a big display, but when she said something, you knew it was pure gold." Of such is the kingdom of heaven.

I'm happy to report that tradition and legends have grown around Martha over the centuries, and organizations too. You won't be surprised to learn that she has been named the patron saint of cooks and housewives; July 29 is designated as her day. The Dutch Renaissance paintings often portrayed her as a cook or as a housekeeper with a key ring. The key ring pleases me very much; after all, if Peter is spoken of as holding the keys to the kingdom on the basis of his announcement of the lordship of Christ, Martha ought also to have a key ring for her equally impressive statement. The artists may have limited her keys to the kitchen; well, if the biblical story finds a grand climax at a heavenly banquet (see Revelation 19:9), I'll be glad for Martha to have the keys to the kitchen.

In some instances I suspect Martha has been both used and misused. In England there were Martha Organizations for the domestic workers in the great manses and guesthouses. On the one hand, such an organization added a dignity to the work; on the other hand, perhaps it was also used by some to restrain further ambition. England also had for a time a Martha Movement, organized by women who were opposed to the emancipation of women.[1] I walk through this ground carefully. On the one hand, no teaching of the Christian faith is more practical and magnificent than the principle of servanthood; but on the other hand, we must be very sure that we don't get so enthusiastic about the servant-ministry of others that we're quite happy for them to be in that role—forgetting that it is a role to which all of us are called. I have been party to conversations that marveled at the willing and sacrificial spirit of a given person while being quite willing to let the individual continue in that role. Martha is to be emulated as well as admired.

Meister Eckhart, the great scholar and Christian mystic of the late Middle Ages, was so taken with the qualities he saw in Martha that he portrayed her as the ideal woman, even more than Mary. This is quite fascinating, since Eckhart taught as a goal of the Christian life a total detachment from worldly matters. One could well portray Martha as the most worldly of saints, the woman whose work in the kitchen kept her from enjoying her sister's privileged position at the feet of Jesus. Eckhart saw her otherwise.

And he was not alone. Over the centuries artists have gone from depicting Martha in the Dutch Renaissance style of kitchen worker to presenting her as an example of a life devoted to Christ through prayer and ministering to others. Fra Angelico painted her into the scene in the Garden of Gethsemane; while the three disciples sleep nearby, Martha is alert and praying. Later legends pictured her as a vegetarian, leading an ascetic life, becoming the head of a convent, always preaching and healing the sick, even to the point of raising a dead person who had longed to hear her preach.

But with all the legends that have grown around her, Martha's best story is just in being Martha. She was the soul of hospitality, a bit flustered on occasions and able to succumb to self-pity, a quality most of us know something about. But she wanted terribly to please her Lord. And when the showdown came at the death of her brother, Lazarus, she spoke with the language and perhaps the authority of Peter. She knew her Lord, in all his glory. I can't think of any apostles who did better.

CHAPTER FOUR

Mary,
the Extravagant

Scripture Reading: John 12:1-8

So we have Martha the disciplined and Mary the extravagant, and they are sisters. Almost surely you have met them somewhere besides in the Bible. In truth, they're fairly common siblings. Nevertheless, when we see them, we almost always shake our heads in disbelief as we say, "Can you believe that they're sisters?"

In our contemporary culture, where we look to psychology for so many explanations, someone will surely conclude that Martha was an *enabler,* that it was her disciplined nature and its accompanying readiness to pick up after Mary that made Mary the kind of person she was, a woman extravagant with money, with emotions, and with life. And there may be some truth to such a theory.

But it's hard to say, because so many elements go into the shaping of our personalities and the conduct that comes from them. Most of us feel that where heredity is concerned, we get our inclinations not only from our mothers and fathers but also from grandparents and assorted aunts and uncles. And we seem strangely selective in these influences, so that where one sibling draws upon a conservative grandmother, another chooses that wayward aunt—even if it's an aunt she's never met.

Modern studies also suggest that birth order plays a significant part in the nature of our personalities. The oldest child has decided traits, as does the youngest; and now we know that the middle children—especially those in a strategic middle—are a class unto themselves. None of these roles is ironclad, because so many other elements contribute to our makeup. But put together parental upbringing, peculiar hereditary contributions, and the influences of particular times—economic depression or prosperity, war, plagues, a change in the neighborhood—and the total becomes in some instances an angelic recipe and in others a witches' brew.

Well, it was neither extreme for Martha and Mary, but they *were* different. We've already talked about Martha, so let's turn our attention now to Mary. We can be almost sure that she was the younger sister and perhaps the youngest member of the family. Martha wouldn't have been the leader in the household in that first-century, highly structured world if she hadn't been the oldest. First children and second or last children can both be spoiled, but they'll be spoiled in different ways. Martha was spoiled to feel her importance and her significance—that is, to know that she was necessary; Mary, I venture, was spoiled to feel her freedom.

It's clear that Mary enjoyed her freedom. In Martha's story we learned that Mary gravitated to freedom and the chance to sit at Jesus' feet as naturally as Martha gravitated to responsibility and the chance to prepare a meal. The little scenario that unfolded in our previous reading was surely not the first in which Mary was going her happy way while Martha kept accounts, made meals, and maintained order. And when Martha appealed to Jesus to bring some discipline into Mary's life, I don't think it was the first time the situation was an issue between the two women; it's simply that in this case Martha called on an outside authority for help. It was a call that, I have a feeling, she may at other times have directed to their brother, Lazarus.

Now we've come to a crucial time in the life of our Lord—six days before the Passover, the Gospel writer dates it, and only a few days before what we now refer to as Holy Week. Jesus is once again in "Bethany, the home of Lazarus, whom he had raised from the dead" (John 12:1), a home where he was uniquely at ease. And once again a meal is involved. This time we're told that the little family "gave a dinner for him," which suggests some sort of celebratory occasion. We know the disciples were there, and perhaps other people from the village. And we're not surprised that "Martha served" (John 12:2). Serving meals may sometimes have become burdensome to Martha, but she did it well, and because she did, I'm sure she found pleasure in it.

And Mary? Well, Mary was about to become extravagant. She took a large bottle of "costly perfume made of pure nard" and poured it out on Jesus' feet. It was a wild thing to do, expensive, unrestrained, and altogether inappropriate. Judas, the treasurer of the apostles and a man who knew the market well (I fear Oscar Wilde's phrase would have fit him: "A man who knows the price of everything and the value of nothing"), made a quick estimate. The perfume was worth three hundred denarii. That was a first-century way of saying, "This represents a working man's wages for an entire year" (see John 12:15). Translate this into even our minimum wage, and we're talking in the language of our day of something in excess of ten thousand dollars. Sometimes while waiting for a haircut I'll pick up one of these magazines that contain five pages of opulent advertising for each page of content, and where everything seems grossly overpriced; even in such a magazine, I can't imagine a perfume costing such a price.

It's the kind of perfume, of course, that you touch carefully to an earlobe or perhaps to the forehead or the base of the neck. The slightest touch will make scent enough for people of taste. But at this moment Mary isn't a person of taste. She is a woman of adoring gratitude, who in her single-minded devotion has lost all sense of time, place, and money. She only knows that she must pay the debt of love.

Mary's nature was such that she didn't really need a particular reason for gratitude. Her nature went out looking for reasons. But she had an extraordinary reason just now, because some days or weeks earlier Jesus had raised her brother, Lazarus, from the dead. This no doubt played a part in what Mary did; but I repeat, Mary was entirely in character at this moment. She was an extravagant personality, and she had found the person who merited extravagance such as hers.

Now this perfume-pouring would of itself have been enough, but Mary had only begun. When I say she was extravagant, I hope you realize I'm speaking of far more than money. Money, if you have it, is the least form of extravagance because, as they say, there's always more where that came from. But when you give *yourself* away, that's quite another matter. Mary now began to wipe Jesus' feet with her hair. It was an act of such complete self-abandonment that it would mark her in the community for the rest of her life. They would never mention her name again without a reference—by story, by gesture, or by innuendo—to this day. Mary's gift of perfume was large, but not to be compared with the gift of herself.

But if Mary would be remembered in Bethany for her unlikely conduct, the Gospel writer lets us know that something else was going on. "The house was filled," he writes, "with the fragrance of the perfume" (John 12:3). John's Gospel is marked by the author's use of double meanings. In the story of Jesus and the woman of Samaria (John 4:1-42), water has both its customary physical meaning and a spiritual meaning. When Jesus heals the blind man (John 9), blindness is both a physical and a spiritual issue. So, here, when John tells us that the fragrance of the perfume filled the house, he is dealing with more than olfactory matters. Some of the theologians in the early centuries of the church said this meant that the whole body of the church experienced the fragrance of Mary's deed. I think John wanted his readers to understand that the loveliness of this act of generosity invaded all of life. Nothing could shut it out; nothing could diminish its sweet, strong, irresistible influence.

Jesus himself said as much. In Matthew's record of the story, Jesus says, "Truly I tell you, wherever this good news is proclaimed in the whole world, what she has done will be told in remembrance of her" (Matthew 26:13). So it is that we write about it today nearly twenty centuries after the event.

But I suspect that no beautiful deed has ever been done but that someone has found fault in it. As we have already noticed, as John tells the story, Judas complains about the waste. Matthew, in his account, spreads the fault around; he writes, "But when the disciples saw it, they were angry" (26:8), insisting the money could have been used better in feeding the poor. I think Jesus saw this complaint for what it was. The disciples were not at this moment so moved by concern for the poor as they were upset by the woman's conduct. I don't think the disciples were unfeeling for the poor, but neither do I hear them expressing such a concern at any other time. To be honest with you, in my years as a pastor I heard people criticize almost every kind of gift by suggesting "better ways" to use the money. And if I had been more outspoken (and, in fact, more honest) I would have said in many instances, "If you want money to be used that way, why don't you give it?" At times there is something in us that refuses to rejoice in an act of kindness or generosity; we feel instead a necessity to diminish it. And usually this is because by diminishing the gift of another we excuse our own parsimonious conduct.

I think Mary often experienced this kind of criticism. After all, she appears in the gospel story only three times, and in two of her appearances she is criticized by someone for the way she showed her loyalty and love for her Lord. And, of course, the criticisms had their merit. When her sister, Martha, complained that Mary should be helping with hospitality rather than sitting at the Master's feet, she had a case. And when Judas and other disciples said there were more practical ways to use her money, some substantial logic was on their side.

Indeed, perhaps one of the major lessons we can learn from Mary and her critics is that there is more than one way to serve the Master and more than one way to show our love for him. And furthermore, one is not necessarily better than the other. Let me say, for instance, that Mary was not the only extravagant person in her family. Martha was pretty extravagant when she labored at the dinners she served our Lord. But her extravagance was within more conventional bounds, and it's easier to understand because it dealt with necessities such as food, and with the normal structures of hospitality. Mary's display was outside the rules; indeed, to be honest, it was outside common sense.

Let me interrupt the story for a moment to observe that apparently neither Martha nor Lazarus joined in the criticism of their sister; at least there is no such record, and I'm quite sure it would be part of the account if such criticism had been made. Is it simply that the two older siblings had gotten to a place where nothing Mary did could shock them? Or were they caught up with her in the ecstasy of extravagant devotion?

Is there a place for Mary's kind of giving and loving? Absolutely. There ought to be occasions in our giving and in our loving when we abandon all sense of logic and propriety. When Saint Francis of Assisi ran and kissed the leper, he lacked good taste and good sense, but he demonstrated extravagant love. Saint Francis knew that this man—accustomed to constant rebuffs and avoidance—needed to be embraced. And come to think of it, perhaps Francis also knew that he himself needed to be violently delivered from himself, even if only for a moment. I submit that in that moment of running to the leper, Francis was once again converted. In embracing the leper he embraced Christ in a new way.

I tend usually to be a reasonable person, reflecting my northern European roots. But I need to forget logic sometimes and throw perfume in the air. Halford Luccock, for many years the professor of homiletics at Yale Divinity School, once made a playful defense of the Christmas song "The Twelve Days of Christmas." He suggested that we too often give people what they need, like a pair of socks or a new kitchen utensil, when we'd do well to give them some maids a-milking and a partridge in a pear tree. Now and then there's something to be said for reckless loving and reckless giving.

Sometimes this reckless loving has a pretty serious face. I remember a woman into her seventies who was still taking care of a son who was severely limited from birth with cerebral palsy. Her love for the boy was lived out extravagantly. I think too of some people who have gone to perilous assignments for Christ: Believe me, they have poured perfume in the air that compares with Mary's. It is reckless and self-forgetting. And sometimes they've gotten their criticism too. I've heard folks say of them, "They could work in *this* country too. We need nurses and doctors *here*, you know."

Sometimes love just insists on using its perfume in abandon. I've noticed that when it does, the fragrance has a way of filling the house—not only the extended residence of geography but also the house of time. So it is that we get the fragrance still today from Mary's extravagance and from other extravagant souls, such as Francis of Assisi, and William and Catherine Booth, and Mother Teresa. The fragrance spreads in ways that are altogether astonishing. Astonishing, I guess, in the same way that such acts of love are astonishing and beyond our patterns of calculation.

I'm impressed that Jesus wasn't embarrassed by Mary's unrestrained conduct. In no way did he suggest that her act was inappropriate or untimely or out of place—though all three criticisms could have been justified. But of course! Because how could the Christ, who within days would go to the cross for our human race, be embarrassed by an extravagant act? Was there ever in all of history an occasion where more costly ointment was poured out more unreservedly, more irrationally, and more extravagantly than at the cross?

And I don't think I'm stretching a matter when I see something special in Jesus' saying that her gift was "for the day of my burial." As a pastor I presided at more than one funeral where generosity was shown in the casket and flowers that ought to have been shown when the person was living; it seemed the tears were shed a bit late. Nicodemus—kindly, generously, and perhaps somewhat repentantly—brought spices to Jesus' burial place (see John 19:39). Mary

46

did so while our Lord was still living. Her extravagance was on time.

Mary was an extravagant sort, no doubt about it. Our culture could argue that some of this quality was written into her genetic code. But when she made Jesus Christ her Lord, a new quality came into whatever may have been part of her natural disposition. Now her inclination toward extravagance found a magnificent purpose.

But remember this: Above all, Mary gave herself. This was her ultimate extravagance. And this possibility is open to all of us—whatever our place in the family order, whatever the extent of our financial resources, whatever our natural inclination to restraint or generosity. God's call is to give *ourselves*. Extravagantly.

CHAPTER FIVE

The Mighty Widow

Scripture Reading: Mark 12:41-44

The whole incident couldn't have lasted more than five minutes, but it is significant enough that both Mark and Luke tell the story. A two-word phrase describing the issue of the story has become part of our common speech; you'll find it in any good-sized dictionary, and thousands of people use it daily without realizing they're making a biblical reference. Let me introduce you to the Mighty Widow, a woman from the time of the apostles who had her own kind of apostolic power.

As I just said, she was a widow. To us, that speaks of loss and loneliness; but for her, in her time and place, it meant much more. She lived in a world where widows were almost completely dependent upon others. There was no possibility for paid employment and very little for independent financial status. In her culture, a widow almost surely had to rely upon a son, a brother, or even a brother-in-law for the simplest basics of existence. Otherwise she would have had to throw herself upon charity, or worse, become a street beggar.

The New Testament tells her story with disarming brevity. First, however, let me give some background. The time of this incident is the countdown time in Jesus' life. He and his disciples are headed toward Jerusalem for events that will culminate in Jesus' arrest, trial, and crucifixion. Jesus knows that this is so. As Luke's Gospel puts it, Jesus "gathered up his courage and steeled himself for the journey to Jerusalem" (Luke 9:51, *The Message*). You can feel the tension in the chapters that follow. You sense that Jesus is increasingly impatient with superficiality and hypocrisy, and with "convenient" religion. There's nothing convenient about the path Jesus is taking, this path that leads to the cross; and you can sense his holy insistence in the parables he speaks along the way and in the intensity of his encounters.

In the verses just preceding the widow's story, Jesus denounced the all-too-typical religious leaders of the day: They parade about, he said, courting adulation, looking for places of prominence on public occasions. "They devour widows' houses and for the sake of appearance say long prayers" (Mark 12:40). Then a poignant scene caught Jesus' eye, a scene that seemed to dramatize what he had just said.

There in the part of the temple compound known as "the Court of the Women" were thirteen collection boxes. They were called "the Trumpets" because of their shape. Contributors had to announce their gifts to a priest standing at the spot; then, as the gift was dropped into the metallic container, the sound of the coin would ring out.

As Jesus and the disciples watched, a number of well-to-do people marched forward and dropped in their sizeable contributions. These givers were impressive, and so were their gifts. I see them in beautifully tailored garments, some of them in the company of their servants. A few chose to be relatively unobtrusive, but many made an unabashed display of their giving. But they were giving impressive sums, and human curiosity, for better or worse, made observers wonder which one might exceed them all.

I'm quite sure Jesus' disciples were a bit in awe of what was going on. Most of them were backcountry fellows, and they were drinking in the glamour of the big city, Jerusalem. There hadn't been much wealth or ostentation in their simple lives, so they couldn't help standing agape at some of the larger gifts. Then, suddenly, Jesus broke in on their reverie.

I see him touching the arms of several, drawing them close so he can have their full attention. "Look at that woman." I'm sure the disciples look right past her. She's dressed plainly, in widow's weeds—mourning clothes— inconspicuous among the tailored and favored. She had waited, I think, until she could approach a priest quietly, so others wouldn't hear the size of her gift. She had whispered the information to him, the way one does when you've slipped into a store that is beyond your means and you've dared to ask the price of a simple article. You speak so cautiously that the insensitive clerk answers loudly, "Pardon me, I didn't hear what you said." And if you are young, he probably adds, "Speak up, young lady!" Something like that, I think, happened to this woman. And even when she repeated her message for the priest, he couldn't understand her. No matter, she was already hurrying away, leaving the priest muttering to himself.

"That woman," Jesus said. "Look at her." The disciples were disappointed and confused. She was nothing to look at, just a quite ordinary, obviously poor widow.

"I tell you," Jesus continued, "this widow put more in the offering box than all the others." Now Jesus had their attention. Perhaps they thought that they'd missed something, that she was actually a wealthy dowager who was traveling incognito. Or more likely, that Jesus was once again talking the peculiar nonsense that so often frustrated them.

In truth, the woman had given two small coins, a coin so small it was known as a lepton, which means literally "thin one." The two coins added up to about a penny. In the widow's style of life, these two coins were roughly enough to buy the woman her next very meager meal.

So now Jesus went on to explain what had happened. "The others," he said, nodding toward the comfortably appointed, "put in what they had to spare of their riches; but she, poor as she is, put in all she had—she gave all she had to live on" (Mark 12:44 TEV).

I have to tell you that I envy this woman, and I dare to suggest that you too might well envy her. She has a decided edge on me. I mentioned earlier that this story has put a phrase into our language, including a place in the dictionary: "widow's mite." I see her as the Mighty Widow. She came one day to a temple court, where people of wealth, power, and influence were parading their strength; and she walked off with the prize. The Lord of glory—the only judge whose opinion really matters—watched her and said, "She's given more than anybody." She wins.

Jesus based his judgment on a simple equation. Most of us judge contributions to church and worthy causes by their size; Jesus judged them by what the person had left after the contribution. He judged, not by what the gift was worth in the marketplace, but by what it had cost the giver. I suspect that this may indicate what the gift is worth in the heavenly exchange.

Let me spell it out this way. Suppose one of the men who came to the temple that day was worth the equivalent in our culture of one hundred thousand dollars. That isn't an unreasonable figure by any means. And suppose he gave ten thousand dollars. If I had been a supervising priest at the setting, I would have been delighted and impressed. But as Jesus viewed things, such a contributor would trail far behind the

Mighty Widow. Specifically, by giving ten thousand dollars out of his one hundred thousand, he has given ninety thousand less than the widow! He still has ninety thousand left, and she has nothing. That's why Jesus was so impressed by her gift. She had given ninety thousand dollars, so to speak, more than the rich man! How do you out-give someone like that? Do you see why I call her the "Mighty Widow"?

And do you see why I envy her? Between you and me, I tithe my income; I've done so since I was ten years old. And in truth, now I give more than a tithe. But I do so from a place of comparative comfort. I have a pension program. We live in a lovely home—not ostentatious, but with enough bathrooms to bless my sense of privacy. We can eat out. The Depression-bred-boy who still occupies the back of my mind gets uncomfortable when the bill is large, even though I can afford it; but the point is, I *can* afford it. To be honest, I wouldn't know how to begin to compete with this Mighty Widow. I know, I know: She lived in a different world from ours, a decidedly simpler world. But having said that, I must go on to say that this widow compels me to do more than I'm doing. After all my rationalizing about the difference in our two worlds and times, she nevertheless shames me into giving more than I'm giving.

We sometimes are told to "give until it hurts." That would be difficult for many of us. Well, there are exceptions of course, because when it comes to giving, some folks have a very low threshold of pain. They hurt easily. But it's hard for most of us to give until it hurts, because we give out of our abundance. And because we're so accustomed to our comfort, we don't really realize the extent of our abundance.

But on what grounds do I see a kind of apostolic power in this Mighty Widow? The scene I've just described is the only place she appears in our Bible, although as I said earlier, both Mark and Luke tell her story. In any event, we have no record that this woman ever really followed Jesus. We can romanticize about it; a novelist could probably weave a full-scale scenario out of a few facts and much imagination. But, of course, we have no substantial factual data. At best we might simply speculate as to how this woman, poor as she was, managed to live another day and another week.

But I see her as a person of extraordinary power, high in the ranks of God's purposes. I feel our Lord would say of her, "Of such is the kingdom of heaven." She is the meek, who will inherit the earth. She is the kind of person on whom our Lord intended to build the kingdom of heaven. And if you wonder how I dare to say such a thing, let me remind you that Jesus said, "The kingdom of heaven is like a mustard seed that someone took and sowed in his field; it is the smallest of all the seeds, but when it has grown it is the greatest of shrubs and becomes a tree, so that the birds of the air come and make nests in its branches" (Matthew 13:31-32). The Mighty Widow is a mustard-seed kind of person, for sure. If you'll forgive my pun, she is the kind of person whom some of us today would describe as being "a little seedy looking."

And if you think I'm making this up, just check your dictionary; *seedy* means "shabby," or "shabbily dressed." She qualifies, this mustard-seed of a woman. But watch out for that mustard seed. Jesus is telling us that the mustard seed may be just a mite, to be held carefully between thumb and forefinger, but it is *mighty.*

And if Jesus' listeners didn't get the kingdom message by that parable, "He told them another parable: 'The kingdom of heaven is like yeast that a woman took and mixed in with three measures of flour until all of it was leavened'" (Matthew 13:33). That's the language of the Mighty Widow. What our modern translations call "yeast" was then known as "leaven." It was a tiny piece of fermented dough. Three measures of flour, in Jesus' day, was enough to feed a fairly large family. Baked by itself, the flour was flat, hard, and unappealing; but mixed with leaven, the dough swelled up into porous, enticing bread. That's the kind of woman this widow was.

Something else strikes one too. As I said, leaven was fermented dough. As such, it was seen as being ritually unclean, and of itself unappealing. But when given a chance to do its thing, it made a flat piece of dough into an appetizing meal. Such was the widow: easily dismissed by a culture that found her a burden, lacking the natural appeal of the self-sufficient. But she, Jesus said, gave more than them all! There was an ugly flatness to the comfortable giving of the well-to-do, but a blessed bounteousness to the widow's mite. I hear the

Master saying, "She's my kind of people. Of such is the kingdom of heaven."

Because that's the way it is, you know. I believe the kingdom of heaven has been built more on Mighty Widows than on Contented Possessors. I speak from the prejudice of experience. I was nineteen years old, serving as student pastor of a tiny congregation in a town on the edge of the Ozark Mountains. We worshiped in a feed store; the checkerboard design on the front was a regular reminder of our origins. Then we got news that the building was to be sold in a few months.

What to do? I was only nineteen and was as unaware of reality as a teenager is usually inclined to be. While others my age were exercising that sense of indestructibility on motorcycles and what that generation called The Thriller at the amusement park, I was making plans to build a church. And to show that unreality isn't limited to teenagers, that pathetic little congregation went along with me. We would use fieldstone for building materials. Labor was cheap. We had a vacant lot. Away we went!

But one Sunday, only two weeks before our announced building dedication, a loyal deacon came to me. He was as unimpressive as the Mighty Widow, and the brother who accompanied him was even less impressive. "Pastor," he said, "we don't have the money to pay another week's salary to the stonemason." He didn't have to tell me that we had no credit rating; for us, it was cash or nothing. Then, as my face grew dark, his face suddenly brightened. "I know what we can do," he said. "I have a charge account at the grocery store. I'll ask the grocer if I can borrow on my account." He did, and we finished the church. And the Mighty Widow won again.

A longtime friend of mine is the administrator for a number of United Methodist retirement communities in the eastern part of the United States. He called recently just to marvel at something he had discovered. His consortium is in a major fund-raising campaign. "You know what I've found, Ellsworth? Except for two gifts, all of our largest contributors are people who never made more than twenty thousand dollars a year. But they lived frugally, saved, and then gave it all to us." The Mighty Widow would understand that. So would the Mighty Savior.

And what is true financially is, if anything, even truer in other matters of the kingdom. Billy Sunday was the greatest soul winner of several decades of the twentieth century. He came to know Christ, however, through a virtually unknown street preacher in Chicago. Or think of England, in the previous century. Charles Haddon Spurgeon was without doubt the most popular preacher in London in the late nineteenth century (indeed, his sermons were telegraphed weekly to America for newspaper publication). But where did his faith journey begin? One snowy Sunday morning Spurgeon chanced as a teenage boy into a Primitive Methodist church, fifteen people present, the pastor unable to get there, so "a thin man with no pretence to education, who could hardly read the Bible aright" served as a substitute preacher—and

Spurgeon gave his life to Christ. The rest, as they say, is history. And eternal history at that.

I'm all for becoming as able as possible (that's why I teach in a seminary), and I'm ready to accept your millions for the work of God's kingdom; just give me a call. But I get the strange feeling, again and again, that God seems to delight in using the Mighty Widows of our world. It isn't that God is prejudiced toward the helpless, except as the helpless give more room for divine working. It's just that people who give their all, whether it is money, personality, or talent, are powerful beyond all human measure. There's an indefinable element here. Call it grace, call it the work of the Holy Spirit, call it a miracle; I only know that the best history of the church is written in little names.

Mighty little names. I suppose I should write a disclaimer at the conclusion of this chapter, because I have written it with a prejudice. I've told the story elsewhere so I won't repeat myself here, but it was a mighty woman who taught me what to do with my money. She wasn't a widow; she was a woman who never married. She was my Sunday school teacher when I was in the sixth grade, and she taught me to tithe. I wouldn't have a lifetime of financial investments in divine projects around the world if it weren't for her. So if you want, you can discount my enthusiasm for the Mighty Widow, but you'll never convince me. I've met one of her spiritual descendants, and I owe her too much to remain silent. I know apostolic power when I see it, and the Mighty Widow had it.

CHAPTER SIX

The Anonymous Evangelist

Scripture Reading: John 4:7-29, 39-42

Ididn't intend to include this woman in our book. Not because I don't like her, but because I like her too much. Several years ago I included her in another book, and I have preached about her more than several times. I like her spunk, her ability to rise up when life has put her down, and her magnificent witness to our Lord. But with my already having written about her, and with there being more great women than I could include in one short book, I decided to skip her.

But she has forced me to alter my plans. I suspect this is because the same intensity and persuasiveness that made her so tenacious when she was living still carry through when I look at her in the pages of John's Gospel. But she is anonymous.

I'm speaking of the woman of Samaria. The story of her encounter with Jesus is one of the longest in the New Testament, but we're never told her name. Someone with a sarcastic sense of humor might say, "With her having had five husbands, maybe nobody could remember her last name." Perhaps. Or perhaps even people in the early church were a little embarrassed by her, so the Gospel writer could never get this detail. Or perhaps she herself gloried in her anonymity. I can hear her saying, "You may forget my name, but you'll always remember what I did, and what I said, and how I said it."

I could name her "The Woman Who Wouldn't Give Up." When she told Jesus, "I have no husband," he quickly answered, "You are right in saying, 'I have no husband'; for you have had five husbands, and the one you have now is not your husband" (John 4:17-18). Our first inclination is to think her an unstable person at best and an immoral one at worst. But I see something else. I remember that in the first-century world a man could get a divorce simply by declaring his intention. Hillel, perhaps the most noted interpreter of Jewish law at the beginning of the first century, allowed that a man could seek divorce if his wife spoiled a dish of food, or if she spoke disrespectfully of her husband's family in his hearing, or if she spoke loudly enough to be heard in the next house—which is to say, almost any reason sufficed. Perhaps the woman of Samaria was not able to conceive; in a world where children were a kind of measure of immortality and where it was assumed women were at fault if conception didn't occur, it's altogether possible that this woman was repeatedly divorced because of presumed infertility.

Or to be candid, perhaps the divorces occurred because she was a bit too outspoken and clever to get along in a "man's world." Her conversation with Jesus indicates that she wasn't hesitant to express an opinion—and to a man and a stranger, at that. Men may have found her fascinating and attractive at a distance and hard to live with at first hand. To put it another way, a man would have needed a strong ego to cope with this woman, and men aren't always that secure.

In any event, I'm disposed to look at her five divorces and her live-in arrangement with compassion: the divorces, because they weren't necessarily her fault—particularly if infertility was the issue—and her living in an unmarried state because there were virtually no means of lawful employment for a woman in a typical first-century village. To live with a man unmarried was at least preferable to becoming a woman of the street.

I'm saying that I admire her for bouncing back, for not giving up on life or on herself. I'm not endorsing multiple marriages in principle, and I'm surely not endorsing living with someone out of wedlock. But I'm glad that when one man put her out, she didn't take her life or sell it out to prostitution; she tried again. And again. And—well, you get the idea. There was a tenacious quality in this woman of Samaria.

I could also title this chapter "The Woman Who Wouldn't Be Put Down." I listen with delight as she engages in conversation with our Lord: I am delighted for our Lord because he isn't put off by her, and delighted by the woman for her intellectual toughness and her street smarts. They meet—some would say by chance, others would say by providence—at a well. The woman is no doubt surprised to see anyone there because it's noontime, and in that climate people didn't come for water at noon. She is still more surprised to find a man there; wells more often were visited by women. The man was particularly surprising because he was Jewish, and Jews generally avoided Samaria. But the greatest surprise was still to come. The man spoke to her. In their culture men didn't speak to women in public places, and most surely a Jewish man wouldn't speak to a Samaritan woman.

The woman may have been surprised, but she wasn't at a loss for words. When Jesus asked for a drink of water, she quickly took charge of the discussion: "How is it that you, a Jew, ask a drink of me, a woman of Samaria?" (John 4:9). Jesus answered, "If you knew the gift of God, and who it is that is saying to you, 'Give me a drink,' you would have asked him, and he would have given you living water" (John

64

4:10). At this point most of us, seeing the peculiar turn the conversation was taking, would have slipped out of it as quickly as possible. But this woman is an instinctive theologian. She's captured by Jesus' phrase "the gift of God"; she knows she's talking with either a holy man or a charlatan, and she intends as quickly as possible to know which.

Her answer to this came in a strange way. She hadn't told Jesus anything about herself, but he suddenly noted that she had had five husbands and was now living with someone who was not her husband. Just that quickly the woman concluded that Jesus was a prophet. But although she was impressed that Jesus knew about her, she wasn't undone. Since he was a prophet, she wanted to ask him a theological question that had bothered her for a long time. As a Samaritan, she had pondered one of the long-standing points of issue between Jews and Samaritans: Where should people worship—in the temple on Mount Gerizim, where the Samaritans worshiped, or in Jerusalem, the location of the Jewish temple? The answer Jesus gave her is still the most significant summary of worship to be found anywhere: "God is spirit, and those who worship him must worship in spirit and truth" (John 4:24).

The woman's responses may seem disconnected, but that's because we aren't inside this woman's mind, and we haven't followed her spiritual pilgrimage. In most discussions between two people there are at least two logical plot lines at work, since two persons are talking; and there can be three or four plot lines, if one of the persons is confused. That's why we so easily misunderstand, or why we sometimes say, "That isn't what I was talking about," to which our friend replies, "It's what I thought we were talking about." So it is that the woman now says, "I know that Messiah is coming. When he comes, he will proclaim all things to us" (John 4:25). If this response seems to us to be a non sequitur, it's because we don't know the spiritual hunger of this woman. She knows that when the Messiah (the Christ) comes, all the pieces will come together and everything will be right. Jesus' answers make her think about the Messiah. Jesus understands what is going on in this woman's soul, so he reveals to her what otherwise he has shrouded in silence: "I am he, the one who is speaking to you" (John 4:25-26).

"Just then," the Gospel writer tells us, "his disciples came." It seems like an unfortunate interruption, like that special moment during a restaurant conversation when there should be no intrusion and the server stops to ask, "Are you enjoying our asparagus?" In truth, the disciples came at a good moment. Providential, let us say. The woman needs time and solitude to process the discussion she's been having. She "left her water jar"—the matter that brought her to the well just a little while ago—"and went back to the city" (John 4:28).

And there she became an evangelist. We're likely to see this woman as without standing in her community. Preachers and storytellers often suggest that the reason she was coming after water at midday is that she preferred to come when others weren't there. If so, she recovered quickly from this reluctance after her visit with Jesus. As the Gospel writer puts it, "She said to the people, 'Come and see a man who told me everything I have ever done! He cannot be the Messiah, can he?' They left the city and were on their way to him" (John 4:28-30).

Something about this woman was wonderfully persuasive. As I have already indicated, she may well have been ill thought of in her community; even if we read with the best and most sympathetic attitude, we can't help feeling she had an uncertain track record. But when she told people her story, they couldn't wait to follow her lead. Of course, in a sense it was her dubious standing that gave peculiar power to her witness. At seventy, Daniel Webster visited a brother-in-law in New Hampshire, John Colby, whom he hadn't seen in forty-five years. In those days Colby had been an embarrassment to the family with his reckless, godless living, but something had happened to him along the way. Back home, Webster said in amazement, "Why, miracles happen in these later days as well as in the days of old. John Colby has become a Christian."[1] The power of Colby's witness was in the change Webster could see in him. I'm very sure this was something of the secret in the witness of the woman of Samaria.

As John reports it, there were just two parts in the woman's story. First, Jesus was "a man who told me everything

I have ever done." On a surface reading, the woman's words might seem to reflect little more than a psychic novelty. But I'm very sure she meant more than this. After all, Jesus might have gotten this basic data—five husbands and a live-in relationship—from almost anyone in the area. And this was hardly "everything I have ever done." There was more to this woman than her spotted marital history.

And perhaps that's the heart of the matter. Something about this woman's conversation with Jesus revealed to her facets and depths of her own person that she had never known before. I've had conversations like that, and so have you. When I was perhaps sixteen, a good but unconventional woman helped me see my spiritual potential in a way I had never seen it before. I also remember a woman pastor, nearly fifty years ago, who was self-ordained before a small denomination recognized her gifts and ordained her formally; I still remember my conversations with her, not so much for specific words as for a quality of insight. She didn't tell me "everything I ever did," but she gave me a feeling for many things I never knew I could be. I sense something of that sort in the Samaritan woman's testimony about her encounter with our Lord.

The second part of her story—"He cannot be the Messiah, can he?"—has several interesting possibilities. Is there a kind of wistfulness here, an uncertainty that seems to be seeking confirmation from her friends? Is this woman a seeker, as much as Andrew, James, and John were seekers when they first rose up to follow Jesus? Do I dare put her in the same company as Anna, the woman who was in the temple the day Jesus was presented for dedication by Joseph and Mary? Have I offended your sensitivities when I make this woman of Samaria a spiritual kin to the godly woman who prayed in the temple day and night? I may be overstating the case; I've been known to do that sometimes. But I can't help feeling that the woman of Samaria was a great seeker. After all, she brought up the Messiah question during her conversation with Jesus. It's very clear that the subject was on her mind. Now, after her encounter with Jesus she dares to suggest to her fellow townspeople that she may perhaps have seen the Messiah.

Her phrasing of the issue is really quite artful. She puts the ball in their court, you see. She doesn't insist that she has found the Messiah; she simply throws open the possibility. As a result, she doesn't irritate her friends or put them in a defensive posture. In truth, she gives them the chance to convince her. It's quite a masterful job of selling.

And she succeeds. The townspeople can't wait to see this man who has impressed their friend so much. And when they see him, they are so captivated that they ask Jesus to stay with them, and he stays two more days. I can think of no other instance when Jesus extended a visit in such a fashion.

It's interesting how in one paragraph the Gospel writer gives us three versions of what happened. At first he reports, "Many Samaritans from that city believed in him because of the woman's testimony" (John 4:39). Then he writes, after telling us that Jesus stayed two more days, "And many more believed because of his [Jesus'] word" (John 4:41). Finally, the story ends with the village converts saying to the woman, "It is no longer because of what you said that we believe, for we have heard for ourselves, and we know that this is truly the Savior of the world" (John 4:42).

Which was it? All three. The transforming event began with the woman who told her friends about Jesus. It unfolded when they listened to Jesus for themselves, seeing him firsthand. And it concluded when they believed on the basis of their own experience.

But never forget where, under God, the process began. It was with a woman who came to the well for water, and went away not only without the water she had come to get but without even her pitcher. But with so much else! She had gotten her first full taste of eternal satisfaction. When she came to the well that day, she was rightly at that midday hour in a hot, dry world; but her deeper thirst had been developing for years—God alone knows for how long. I suspect she was a restless woman, probably maligned for the conduct that came from her restlessness. I have met many of her spiritual kin, and I know that society (including the church) usually makes more of the person's restlessness than of the longing behind the restlessness.

So one day she found her Lord and became an evangelist. I don't know what she did after that day or how many other people she led to faith along the way. But on that day she was a magnificent soul winner. And she was anonymous.

That shouldn't surprise us. Let me wager something. When the eternal accounting is done someday, I submit that more transformations will be credited to anonymous evangelists—spouses, siblings, parents, clerks, schoolteachers, pastors in hidden-away places, all of them easily forgotten or unrecognized—than to Billy Sunday, Billy Graham, and Mother Teresa combined. The kingdom of heaven is made by such as these.

CHAPTER SEVEN

Mary Magdalene: When Love Is Greater Than Faith

Scripture Reading: John 20:1-18

So many pictures come to mind when I think of Mary Magdalene, but for me the defining picture is in a phrase from the Resurrection story: "Early on the first day of the week, *while it was still dark*, Mary Magdalene came to the tomb" (John 20:1, emphasis added). "While it was still dark": that phrase captures Mary for me. She had come to

73

the tomb with several other women, Luke's Gospel tells us, bringing the burial spices they had prepared (see Luke 24:1). Their mission was an act of devotion, not a journey of faith. They were coming not to celebrate a resurrection, but to perform one final act of devotion. Jesus had told his followers on several occasions that he must be brought to trial and crucified, and that he would rise again. It seems clear, however, that none of Jesus' followers had heard their Lord clearly enough to grasp the idea of a resurrection, so the crucifixion was the end of it all. But if these women lacked the faith to expect a resurrection, they had the character to remain faithful, so now they had come early to do a task of love.

As John's Gospel tells the story, the emphasis is singularly on Mary Magdalene. We wouldn't guess from John's report that other women were with her. Throughout his Gospel, John is a master dramatist; so at this point in the story he—like a skilled movie director focusing a camera—works so exclusively with the woman of Magdala that the other women are left in the shadows, almost as observers. For those who love deeply there are times when one is alone even while with a group. We feel Mary's aloneness; and when John tells us that she came "while it was still dark," we remember that John's Gospel works often with metaphors of light and darkness, and that he chooses on some occasions to tell us that it is night when we know very well that it is—and that in such instances we understand that he is speaking of something more than the hour of the day. So it is now. Mary comes in the dark.

It was hellish-dark when Jesus first came into Mary's life. She was said to have seven devils. (See Luke 8:1-2.) In our twenty-first century a term like *demonic possession* is easily written off as an expression of superstition from an unscientific age. But we should never take such an intellectually superior position that we don't really hear what is being said. At the very least we should admit, with some humility, that our scientifically approved language is not itself foolproof. I recall that in the mid-twentieth century, when Paul Tillich was perhaps the most admired philosophical theologian in most of the Christian world, he often addressed bodies of psychiatrists to explain his concept of the "demonic." There are mysteries in our human psyche that we do not fully understand and that very likely we never will, because we humans are an exceedingly complex study.

We should remember too that the Scriptures look at all of life from a vantage point different from our own. The Scriptures see the issues of life and of history in their ultimate dimension as a conflict between light and darkness. When a person reacts to life in an utterly irrational and self-destructive way, the biblical writer sees this as demonic. If we see conduct that is completely illogical, we throw up our hands in despair and ask, "How can someone do something like that with his or her life?" A New Testament writer would answer, "Because Satan is involved." The word *Satan* means "adversary"; when in our conduct we become our own adversary, it is not unreasonable to think of such conduct as coming from outside ourselves. I suspect there is no one reading these words who has not at some time observed a friend, an acquaintance, or one's own self doing something so foolish or so destructive that it defies logical description. What is it? A chemical imbalance? A product of our upbringing? An unexplainable desire to self-destruct? The Bible would use the word *demonic*. Some would say that the biblical language is poetic. If so, we should remember that the language of poetry is often closer to the truth of human experience than the language of the laboratory.

Whatever was wrong with Mary Magdalene before meeting Jesus, she was—by popular observation—a hopeless case. The number seven was for the Jews a numerical symbol of completeness, whether the number was used positively or negatively. When believers in biblical times thought of God's Creation taking place in seven days, it was a way of saying that when the job was finished (including the day of rest), everything was complete; it was as good as ever it could be. By contrast, when they said that someone had seven devils, they were saying that the person was as bad off as a person could be. There could be no worse diagnosis than "seven demons."

So Mary Magdalene's was a dark life, indeed. We have no idea how long her condition, whatever its specifics, had existed; we only know that she was as distraught, as confused, as unable to cope with life as a person could be. How dark was her life? As dark as it could be—sevenfold dark.

Then she met her Lord, and in meeting him the measure of light was as intense as once the measure of darkness had been. If those who knew Mary Magdalene saw her previously as possessed of seven devils, they might now see her—if they were to view her with grace comparable to the fear they exercised before—as possessed by seven spirits of goodness and love.

I doubt that her contemporaries did so. We do better understanding profoundly good people after they're dead than in their lifetime. It's very difficult to measure brilliance close up, whether the brilliance is intelligence, creativity, or holiness. I suspect, rather, that Mary's contemporaries were always a bit mystified by her. They may have found Mary the Redeemed as hard to define as once they had found Mary the Lost.

Jesus explained Mary's kind of experience in an event recorded in Luke's Gospel. A woman—"a sinner," Luke says, which probably was intended in that day and context to mean a prostitute—interrupted a dinner party where Jesus was the guest to express her profound devotion to Jesus by anointing him "with an alabaster jar of ointment." Then she "began to bathe his feet with her tears and to dry them with her hair. Then she continued kissing his feet and anointing them with the ointment" (Luke 7:37-38). Some commentators advise us not to associate this story with Mary Magdalene, since the woman's name is not given—although it is natural to make such a connection since the story is followed immediately by a list of women who had been healed of a variety of infirmities, beginning with "Mary, called Magdalene, from whom seven demons had gone out" (Luke 8:1-2). In any event, the incident evoked a teaching moment for Jesus. He noted that those who have been forgiven much show "great love. But the one to whom little is forgiven, loves little" (Luke 7:47). Mary Magdalene, whether or not she was the person in this particular story, knew the kind of experience that made her love Christ unreservedly and follow him with no sense of personal privilege or restraint.

A friend who knows Christ's redemption well and who loves him with extraordinary devotion commented one day, "It's no wonder Mary's freedom from oppression made her run after Jesus for the rest of his earthly life and then after, as well." My friend pondered how miserable Mary had to have been, possessed and obsessed with the demonic. "If the devil, everything that is not God—not good or holy or peaceful—possessed her, can you imagine then the anxiety, the fear, the instability, and the utter irrationality that defined Mary's life for the years she was so possessed?" Most of us have such experiences for only some passing period of fear or loneliness or depression—the kind of experience we can shake off by diversion or by prayer or by conversation with a friend. But what of a life that, day in and day out, is pursued by what seems to be a legion from hell? To be delivered from such terror would make one love in a fashion that "ordinary folk" would think irrational. But ordinary folk aren't equipped to understand—and certainly not to pass judgment on—those who have battled with the irrational.

So I'm very sure people of her time didn't understand Mary Magdalene. They didn't understand her when she was possessed by seven devils, nor could they understand her when she was possessed by gratitude and virtue in commensurate measure. She had suffered deeply, and in the judgment of her culture she had sinned grievously. When I say "in the judgment of her culture," I mean to suggest not that her sin was only a matter of opinion, but that the Gospel writer is reporting on the opinion in which she was held at the time. Sin is in the eye of God, but the degree of sin is more likely to be in the eye of the beholder. I'm not at all sure that God differentiates between sins in the ways we do.

But now Mary was free. If a paralytic were healed, he would leap for joy, and even the dullest onlooker would simply rejoice in the marvel of transformation that made a person who once had been bed-bound to caper now like a child. I wonder why it is that we are not always as understanding when a human being is delivered from soul-paralysis? It is a beautiful thing for a person to be enabled to walk and run; is it anything less for a beleaguered soul to be magnificently free?

Obviously the later first-century Christians understood Mary Magdalene because whenever Matthew, Mark, and Luke mention the company of women who assisted Jesus and the disciples, they always began the listing with Mary. I suspect that her witness was a particularly persuasive one, the kind that believers wanted to hear again and again, and that even contemptuous unbelievers heard with respect. Is her name mentioned first because the other women saw her as their unnamed leader? Very possibly; no doubt there was an appealing, winsome quality in Mary in her wonderfully redeemed state.

Great souls prove their greatness in the darkest of times. In the consuming shadows of the Crucifixion, "standing near the cross of Jesus were his mother, and his mother's sister, Mary the wife of Clopas; and Mary Magdalene" (John 19:25). When Joseph of Arimathea took the body of Jesus to his tomb for burial, "Mary Magdalene and Mary the mother of Joses saw where the body was laid" (Mark 15:47). And so it was that on the morning of the first day of the week, Mary was one of the little group that came early to the tomb, to offer what they intended to be their last gift of devotion. As John's Gospel reports it, when Mary "saw that the stone had been removed from the tomb" (John 20:1), she ran to tell the news to two of the disciples. After they saw the empty tomb, they returned to their homes, apparently in a state of wonder and confusion. But Mary stayed—weeping. "As she wept, she bent over to look into the tomb" (John 20:11). When the two angels sitting inside asked why she was crying (an interesting question to ask at a tomb, is it not?), Mary answered, "They have taken away my Lord, and I do not know where they have laid him" (John 20:13). Mary hasn't come to the tomb in faith to celebrate a resurrection; she has come in love to pay her devotion. There are times and circumstances that faith cannot understand but that prove no hindrance to love. She calls him still her Lord, even though she thinks him dead.

Then our Lord himself appeared to her. She didn't recognize him at first; primarily, I'm sure, because she simply did not expect him—after all, he was dead. Also, she was so distraught by grief that she could see nothing else but that not only was Jesus dead but also his body had been stolen. It was grievous enough that he had been beaten, humiliated, and crucified; now someone was even desecrating his body, an unthinkable act in the mind of a Jew, no matter whose body it might be.

Then it was that Jesus identified himself to her. And so it was that Mary Magdalene was the first recorded witness to the Resurrection; not Simon Peter, the prince of the apostles; not John the beloved; not even Mary the mother of Jesus, but Mary Magdalene. She announced the good news to the disciples; as Saint Augustine saw it, the Holy Spirit made her "the apostle of the apostles."

It isn't surprising that many legends grew around Mary Magdalene. According to one such report she went to Rome after our Lord's ascension and asked for an interview with the emperor, hoping to indict Pilate for his false judgment in Jesus' trial. Another legend said that Mary retired to La

Sainte-Baume, there to live a life of penance for some thirty years. She became the patron saint of the cosmetic industry in the Middle Ages. And of course she was portrayed by unnumbered artists, one of the finest representations being Dürer's woodcut. And of course she has contributed a word to our language: *maudlin,* which means something or someone weakly emotional or unduly sentimental, comes from the British pronunciation of *Magdalen* (Magdalene).

I'm afraid we shouldn't be surprised that Mary Magdalene has repeatedly been interpreted—and misinterpreted—in matters related to sexual conduct. Because her name was associated with sin and because many chose to interpret her seven devils as evidence of extreme sexual misconduct, church bodies adopted her name for the agencies they founded to care for prostitutes or for women who were pregnant out of wedlock. Mary Magdalene seemed to our spiritual ancestors to be the right name for such a ministry of redemption.

This view of Mary has taken on a more salacious quality in recent times. A late twentieth-century musical on the life of Christ portrays a conflicted Mary Magdalene who struggles with the nature of her love for Jesus. A popular contemporary novel builds much of its excitement on the idea that Jesus and Mary were sexually related, and that this information has been hidden from the public. The author of this book notes simply that he is a novelist, which ought to make clear that we're dealing with fiction; but of course the idea is too enchanting for a certain mindset to leave at the fictional level. I venture that no one would be more appalled to hear the name of Jesus associated with sexual misconduct than the woman of Magdala. But I'm equally sure that she would not have been surprised, since in her lifetime she had so often been misjudged.

But no fiction about Mary Magdalene, and not even the wildest legends, can really do justice to her story, a story that needs no adorning. She was a woman who—whatever the particulars of her life—wrestled with terrifying problems, problems so severe that it was as if all hell had set its focus on her. Then she met Christ, and she experienced the kind of deliverance that millions of others through succeeding centuries have also known, in varying measure and form. In a band of unselfishly dedicated women, none of whom was going to get the prominence of Peter, John, or later Paul, she was the most notable. And when her Lord won victory over death, she was—according to all the records—the first to see him.

I repeat, there's no need to add to a story like Mary Magdalene's. One wishes only to have met her.

CHAPTER EIGHT

Mary, the Mother of Mark

Scripture Reading: Acts 12:6-17

The literature of my childhood pictured women as loving and men as courageous. That's why little boys so often are taught not to cry; "Now be a man," someone says. It's a bad saying twice over: for one, because it robs men of the importance of tears, and also because it gives a false picture of women. After all, love and courage do not merely coexist; they belong to each other. In many instances courage is the greatest evidence of love, and would not in fact exist if it were not for love.

I saw so many strong women when I was growing up. I think of the women who worked in the laundry where as a boy I sometimes was the hopper on a delivery truck. The world of that long-ago time was one in which women who worked outside the home were limited almost entirely to teaching, nursing, table-waiting, office work, or various kinds of factory work. A laundry was hot, hard work; and the presses and mangles where women so often worked were especially exhausting. I remember these women as strong women who knew how to laugh in the face of their many adversities. Nearly all of my teachers in public school and in Sunday school were women; they were gracious, intent on civilizing little boys, and very, very strong. I remember the Methodist deaconesses in our town. They were unmarried; they lived in a kind of dormitory; their income was extremely modest; they wore a habit not unlike those that nuns also wore; and they walked fearlessly day after day in neighborhoods where men were known to be afraid. After seventy years, I still remember their names: Miss Humphrey, Miss McCurry, and Miss Beck are part of memory's store. If you don't mind my saying so, they were *tough*. They wore courage as comfortably as they wore their deaconess bonnets. (Reminiscent note: Shessler Hall, where they lived, was across the street from my high school—Central High—and it is still there today, though I don't know how it is used now.)

I say all of this to introduce one of the several Marys who walk through the New Testament story; this one, the mother of John Mark. Some might consider my evidence sparse, but I think it's enough. Her major appearance in the New Testament story is from the earliest days of the Christian faith. This particular story begins ominously: "About that time King Herod laid violent hands upon some who belonged to the church. He had James, the brother of John, killed with the sword" (Acts 12:1-2). Herod was nothing if not a politician. He loved being on the throne; and although he was titled a king, he was actually the ruler of a rather small territory under the power of Caesar. His power in his territory was absolute; but if there were any uprisings or any notable trouble, Caesar would replace him as easily as if he were a chariot driver. So when Herod saw that his persecution of the church pleased the Jewish religious leaders, he arrested Peter too. I'm sure Herod was astute enough to realize that at that point Peter, James, and John were the acknowledged leaders of the church. With James gone, imprisoning Peter—usually the mouthpiece of the movement—was a sweeping gesture of power.

It was enough to make any follower of Jesus tremble. With James gone and Peter in prison, it was probably only a matter of time until Peter too would be executed. And then, almost surely, the authorities would move in on the common folk who made up the mass of the Christian community.

So what were they to do? I don't mean to pass judgment when I say that some of them no doubt forsook the cause at this point. But those who remained knew they needed one another. If ever it was important to have the sustenance of the community, this was it. And yet, to meet was to invite trouble. The authorities would watch for any such gathering. They had no church building, so they would have to meet in someone's home. But who would dare take that chance? If those who came together were in danger, the one who provided the meeting place was in still greater danger. So where did they go? They went "to the house of Mary, the mother of John whose other name was Mark, where many had gathered and were praying" (Acts 12:12).

All of which makes clear that Mary, the mother of Mark, was a very courageous woman. Since no husband is mentioned in the story and no reference is made to Mark's father, we assume Mary was a widow. A twenty-first-century person might answer, "Perhaps she was divorced." In that time and place, if she were divorced, she wouldn't have any property; it would have gone without question to her husband. So we judge her to be a widow.

We can also judge that she almost surely was financially secure—not in the measure of our society, where people have stocks and bonds and properties and businesses, but to a degree that she had a home large enough to hold a fairly sizeable gathering. She was also prosperous enough to have a maid, although this doesn't imply the same level of affluence it might suggest in our day. But compared to most of the first generation of Christians, she was surely more financially secure than the general run of the church.

It's a funny thing about money and financial security. Instead of making people more secure and therefore more ready to take a risk, money tends to make us more conservative. Perhaps it's because we have more to lose, or perhaps it's because we build our resources by not taking too many risks. But Mary contradicts the pattern. She had a great deal to lose—more, certainly, than most of her fellow believers—and especially because, being a woman she would be particularly vulnerable if she lost her resources. Logically, Mary had every reason to avoid trouble. Nevertheless, she allowed the believers to gather in her home. By doing so, she put everything she had on the line.

I don't think I've ever known a true equivalent to Mary, but I'm grateful for Rae Wetmore. She owned a small publishing firm in my hometown, producing plays and declamatory readings for the use of grade school and high-school students. She belonged to a fine, suburban Methodist church; but for several years she drove downtown to teach a boys' class at the Helping Hand Mission, a Methodist church that ministered to the derelicts (as they were known in those days) who circulated along what was known as "lower Fourth Street," and to families on the south and east bottoms—the area of the city that in those days flooded nearly every year. My parents were among the few supporting members of the Mission, but in truth, economically we were not that far removed from the people the church had been established to serve.

I realize now how incongruous it must have been each Sunday when Miss Wetmore (she never married) pulled her stately Packard in front of the Mission. The classroom where we met with her was bare and uninviting, quite different from those in her suburban church. And the class members weren't very prepossessing. I was the only one whose parents also came to church. Nevertheless, of the six or eight boys in the class, two eventually became ministers, one became a college president, and another became a substantial businessman. I lost track of the others, so I may be omitting the best part of the story.

Rae Wetmore never put her life and resources in danger by teaching that mission Sunday school class (although her automobile was a tempting sight in that marginal area). But she made herself an odd figure to her suburban friends. They couldn't understand why she chose to go to lower Fourth Street to teach a class of what in those days were described as ragamuffins, when she could be with her own kind of people teaching some boys and girls who had far more promise. Or at least, so the good folk would have said. Miss Wetmore ostracized herself from much of her natural community by taking the Mission boys into her life and, on some occasions, into her home. She wasn't quite a Mary, but from my prejudiced point of view she was a pretty good facsimile.

Perhaps you noticed the way Luke, the author of Acts, identifies Mary: She is "the mother of John whose other name was Mark" (Acts 12:12). I suppose some might take umbrage at this phrase, feeling that Mary gets her significance from her offspring rather than from her own achievements. But let's put Mary's achievement as a mother into perspective. We don't think we minimize a teacher when we judge her or him by the quality of her or his students; on the contrary, we think this is the ultimate measure of the teacher's success. Personally, I feel I have done no better thing than to raise my children to responsible adulthood. I don't see this as the only accomplishment in my life, but I know of none that gives me greater satisfaction.

And no greater thing can be said for any of us, parents or otherwise, than that we had a positive influence on the next generation. My favorite history professor never won a Pulitzer Prize in history, but he was known for the fact that his students led the way in the number of Pulitzers won. And we knew that this was because of the meticulous savagery he committed on our papers as he sought to make worthy scholars of us. One day after enunciating a demanding standard for our work, he suddenly interrupted himself: "But you want to tell me that I don't follow all these rules myself. You're right. But do you think I'll be satisfied if you prove to be no better than I am?"

So when the writer of the book of Acts identifies Mary as the mother of John Mark, I think he's doing two things. For one, he is helping his readers a generation or more removed from the original happenings to know who this woman was, and the best way to do so was by naming John Mark. At the same time, there's an implicit word: "She must have been quite a woman to produce a son like John Mark."

And who was John Mark? As you probably know, he is the person generally judged to be the author of the Gospel of Mark. As such he was the particular aide and confidant of the apostle Peter. Bible scholars feel that his Gospel was critical to the shaping of the Gospels of Matthew and Luke, as well. In other words, you can hardly read the New Testament without seeing Mark's fingerprints. When you do, remember whose son he is. It isn't by chance that he grew up to be the kind of leader he was.

But it wasn't a path without turning. When you trace John Mark's story through the book of Acts, you know that when he was still a young man, Barnabas and Saul (the latter of whom later became known as the apostle Paul) took him on as their aide. Along the way, John Mark abruptly left the two great leaders to return home. We don't know why. We only know that when Paul and Barnabas began organizing for their next missionary journey, Barnabas—who was related to John Mark and his mother—wanted to take the young man again, but Paul refused because of his disappointment in Mark's earlier conduct. Eventually the two great souls, Paul and Barnabas, split over the issue. One's vote has to go with Barnabas, in light of the later beauty of Mark's life—and also in light of the fact that Paul himself later described John Mark as being "useful in my ministry" (2 Timothy 4:11).

John Chrysostom, the towering fourth-century theologian

and preacher, said that Mark left Barnabas and Paul because he wanted his mother. On the one hand, that's quite possible; and in its own way, whether one likes it or not, that may demonstrate again how strong a woman Mary was. In those youthful years, away from home, John Mark could have been unduly dependent upon her. I know I'm violating some psychological theories in saying so, but I don't think this is one of the world's major faults. On the other hand, it could be that Mark left the older men because his mother had taught him to be so strong and independent that he became restless with the leadership of Paul and Barnabas. The inclination of the young to be impatient with the apparent conservatism of the older is not a twenty-first-century phenomenon; it has always been so, even if in some generations it was successfully cloaked in respect for elders. John Mark may have been doing nothing other than demonstrating the strength his mother instilled in him.

It wasn't easy to be a follower of Jesus Christ in that first century of the Christian faith. If ever there was a body of people open to persecution, they were it. In a peculiar but pragmatic way, it's not surprising that most of the early Christians were persons of modest positions and limited influence, because they were the people with "nothing to lose," so to speak. Perhaps they found it easier to gamble on Christ because they had less to gamble. In any event, they were a magnificent collection of saints-in-the-making, and Mary was one of the greatest.

If we take our faith seriously, it still isn't easy to be a follower of our Lord. When I say this, I intend to draw a distinction between the kind of religion that is a convenience for occasions of need or display and the kind that demonstrates itself in everyday commitment. I am speaking of the kind of faith that makes church membership different from any other social or community obligation. For Mary, it meant opening her home to the possibility of public peril. It meant identifying herself with people who were generally less fortunate than she was and making them her people—and in doing so, taking the risk that she would lose association with persons whose social and economic status was more like her own.

Forgive me if I seem melodramatic, because what I'm about to say is hard fact. There's no doubt some sentiment in it too, but facts often have their sentimental side. I want to say just this: Note that we don't have any knowledge of any of the friends and neighbors Mary may have lost by her acts of courage, by her taking up of the cross of Christ. But we still know Mary's name and her story. And literally billions of persons have been blessed over these twenty centuries because of her son, John Mark. So when you read that Peter, miraculously released from prison, "went to the house of Mary, the mother of John whose other name was Mark, where many had gathered and were praying" (Acts 12:12), know that you are treading on sacred ground. This was a great woman, great in her courage and in the love for Christ in which her courage was born.

CHAPTER NINE

Dorcas:
Worth a Miracle

Scripture Reading: Acts 9:36-42

I spoke recently in a church that had a Dorcas Circle. I've spoken in hundreds of churches over the past half-century, and have read thousands of church bulletins, but I can't recall the last previous time I came upon a Dorcas Circle. But it was only two or three days later, while I was doing research in a book published in 1899, that I came upon this phrase: "The name 'Dorcas,' so familiar to us through those very useful societies in our modern churches which bear it to-day,"[1] and I realized how times have changed.

Dorcas was, indeed, a familiar and popular name in churches near the end of the nineteenth century and early in the twentieth. I think the name won its popularity entirely on its own; as far as I can learn, Dorcas groups thrived not because of something born in the offices of a national church body but because they came from the sort of idea that grew on its own merit.

But ideas and movements and enthusiasms often have their season and are forgotten, and so it seems to be, in some measure, with Dorcas Circles. So too with Dorcas as a given name; I haven't met a woman named Dorcas in more than fifty years. That fact is underlined before my eyes, even as I write, because my computer underscores Dorcas in red, to indicate that it is a misspelling—or in this case, a personal name that isn't included in the quite vast vocabulary of a computer's acceptable terms.

I'm sorry about that, because Dorcas was quite a woman. On the one hand, she was a woman of such significance in her community that those who loved her—and they were many!—thought she was worth a miracle. And apparently, Simon Peter agreed with them; and still more important, so did the Holy Spirit, so that a miracle did in fact occur. This means that Dorcas was a remarkable person, indeed. On the other hand, I know even as I enter into Dorcas's story that you may respond unfavorably to my including her in this book of great women followers of Jesus. I'll take that chance because I believe so much in Dorcas and in what she represents.

Her story comes to us from a time described relatively early in the book of Acts, when the church was young and when miracles were expected. She lived in Joppa, which was a port city located about thirty-five miles from Jerusalem. We know nothing of Dorcas's parents, or whether she was married or had a family of her own. Some scholars speculate that she was a businesswoman, though we have no substantial proof for that idea. I'm fascinated by her name, which the book of Acts chooses to give us in both its Aramaic (*Tabitha*) and Greek (*Dorcas*) forms. Her name meant "a gazelle." We don't know whether this was her given name or whether (like Barnabas, for example; see Acts 4:36) it was what we would today call a nickname, a name given to her by her friends because it seemed to fit. A gazelle is a beautiful creature, lovely in its gracefulness. I can't help thinking the people saw such loveliness in this woman that they called her by a name that sought to capture the beauty they saw in her.

She enters the apostolic story after she has died. I think her death was quite unexpected; the author of Acts says simply, "she became ill and died" (Acts 9:37). Her friends washed her body to prepare her for burial, and they laid her in a second-floor room—whether in her own home or another, the writer doesn't say.

Then something special happened. Some of the people heard that the apostle Peter was in the nearby community of Lydda, so they sent two men to appeal to him, "Please come to us without delay" (Acts 9:38). It appears they didn't tell

Peter why they were bringing him; they simply took him to the upstairs room where the body of Dorcas—perhaps we should use the harsh but true word, her corpse—lay. There Peter found himself surrounded by a gathering of widows, all of whom were weeping "and showing tunics and other clothing that Dorcas had made while she was with them" (Acts 9:39).

Luke, the author of Acts, doesn't tell us what these people said to Peter; he tells us only that they were weeping and showing how much this woman had meant to them. Luke has already told us the kind of woman Dorcas was: "She was devoted to good works and acts of charity" (Acts 9:36). When the widows appear before Peter, they show the medium Dorcas used for her good works: She made clothing.

So Peter excused everyone from the room and knelt down to pray. Then he did a quite extraordinary thing: "He turned to the body and said, 'Tabitha, get up'" (Acts 9:40). Luke then reports rather matter-of-factly that Dorcas "opened her eyes, and seeing Peter, she sat up." Peter, in a gentlemanly turn, "gave her his hand and helped her up," after which he called "the saints and widows" to let them see that the woman they so much loved was again alive (Acts 9:40-41).

I won't comment on the miracle here reported except to note words from the late Theodore Parker Ferris, one of the most esteemed clergy in the Episcopal Church in America during the mid-twentieth century: "Stories like these occur over and over again in the history of early Christianity. They occur too often to allow us to discredit them as fiction."² I am not so interested at this point in the miracle that happened as I am in the story behind it. From a pragmatic point of view the most important thing about a miracle is what may have helped bring it to pass. In this instance, some people cared so deeply for a woman named Dorcas that they dared to solicit help from Peter, the most strategic of the apostles. And something about their earnestness and the case they made got to Peter in such a measure that he didn't settle for a comforting, pastoral word; he was driven to prayer, and his prayer in turn led to a miracle.

So I am impressed that Dorcas was worth a miracle. Of course in the broadest sense, every human being is worth a miracle; our Christian gospel is built on that kind of conviction. But here was a human being whose impress on others was so great that they simply couldn't let her go. I repeat what I said earlier: We don't know clearly what Dorcas's devoted friends and beneficiaries asked of Peter or what they expected from him. It's clear, however, that they were asking for something entirely out of the ordinary and that their appeal was of such a quality that Peter felt compelled to respond with his whole, remarkable faith commitment.

What was so wonderful about Dorcas? "She was devoted to good works and acts of charity." *Devoted*: That word stands out. I have spent my life in the church, both as a boy growing up and in my adult years as a professional church worker, so I know a lot about good works and the people who perform them. They are salt-of-the-earth people. I have known people of this quality, ranging from those who volunteered at rescue missions to those who have served on the boards of hospitals and universities. I admire them all, and I'm satisfied that no one can begin to estimate how much *good* such people do.

But for most such people, good works are a side issue, something they do after they've finished the essential work of making a living and often also after finishing the nonessentials of hobby, recreation, and self-satisfaction. Only rarely is someone *devoted* to good works. I ponder too that Dorcas's devotion was to "good works"; I'm quite sure I have known times in my life and perhaps have seen in the lives of others a commitment that was not really to the good works, but to the impression the good works would make or the favor the good works would win. I don't really mean to be unduly judgmental; I just know from experience that "good works" can flow from a variety of motives. As a result, I am quite in awe of this woman for whom good works were not a side issue and not a means to an end, but quite surely the incisive devotion of her life. William Tyndale, in his translation that laid the foundation for the King James Version of the Bible, said that Dorcas was "full of good works" (Acts 9:36); so full, I dare say, that there was little room left for self or self-seeking.

We have no idea whether Dorcas ever saw Jesus for herself, or whether she was one of the converts who came after our Lord's death and resurrection. While there is no biblical reference to Jesus visiting Joppa, it's altogether possible that Dorcas saw and heard him at some other place. But however it was that Dorcas became a disciple, it's wonderfully clear that she got the message. She was an exemplar of the kind of person Jesus described in his picture of the judgment, when we will be identified by our treatment of "the least of these" (see Matthew 25:31-46). If we take seriously Jesus' teaching in the parable I've just mentioned, we have to say that when Dorcas made clothing for widows and orphans, she was, in the process, clothing her Lord. Perhaps then it isn't surprising that she experienced his resurrection power. Some things that happen in the realm of the spirit are not quite so mysterious as we make them. I submit that there is more logic involved in matters of faith than we sometimes realize. The logic is there if we have the spiritual perception to see it.

But back again to the "tunics and other clothing that Dorcas had made." I'm caught betwixt two trains of thought. On the one hand, sentiment is at work. My mother took pride in being a seamstress. The sound of a sewing machine—in my schooldays, a foot-pedaled one—was part of the music of our home. For my mother, sewing was an art, and a finished dress that hung properly was a holy achievement. So it is enough for me that Dorcas made clothing for the poor; in my scale of values, her nobility is assured.

But on the other hand, times have changed, as they have a tendency to do, and I suspect that some people in our world today see Dorcas as a symbol of those days when women's place in the church was to cook chicken suppers and make clothing for the mission field, while men preached, served as trustees, and generally ran the life of the church. As one who has been teaching preaching for well over a decade, I not only believe in women's leadership in the church, I also wonder how many potentially magnificent preachers and leaders went unheard and undiscovered in those generations when positions of leadership were largely isolated to men.

Nevertheless, I dare to make a twenty-first-century case for Dorcas. I wish there might be a revival of Dorcas societies in our churches, with men encouraged (on proper approval!) to join them. I am utterly sure that the gospel is never more real, never closer to what our Lord intended, than when it is serving the needs of the poor. And while I am fully committed to the struggle for justice that has to be fought out in legislative assemblies and by speeches and petitions, I am just as sure that nothing quite takes the place of love that shows itself in hands-on deeds: "tunics and other clothing." I see no reason why regaining the works of righteousness at one level should mean the abandonment of such works at another level. In our century I want Dorcas to stand with Peter when he challenges the ecclesiastical authority in Jerusalem, but not at the loss of her strategic ministry to the needy. Just let Peter join her there.

And here's a question that continues to fascinate me as I read the story of Dorcas. She is the only person who was so important to the early body of believers that they appealed to the premier leader of the church for help. I've spent my life as a preacher and teacher, so I hate to raise the question, but I wonder: Was there any preacher or teacher in Joppa whose death would have left the community as bereft as the death of Dorcas? Would they have made such a dramatic appeal at the loss of a bishop or any comparable church official? Don't you think it's remarkable that it was Dorcas and her unique yet decidedly ordinary ministry that evoked a miracle?

God knows I don't intend to minimize preaching, teaching, and administration. But it's easy for any of these (perhaps especially administration) to get detached from the heart of the gospel. Because the gospel is not in words, but in deeds; and while nothing can take the place of inspired and anointed words in the communicating of the faith, the words are sounding brass and tinkling cymbals if they are not implemented and fulfilled by love. And love generally puts on its work clothes and rolls up its sleeves.

So here's to Dorcas, who was worth a miracle, because she put hands and feet to the gospel, and she did so with all her heart, with self-forgetting devotion. If I ever run onto a Dorcas Society where I live, I'm going to petition for membership. Since my mother didn't pass her sewing skills to me, maybe I can serve as their delivery agent.

CHAPTER TEN

Lydia,
the Businesswoman

Scripture Reading: Acts 16:11-15, 40

Former President Jimmy Carter has been a Sunday school teacher longer than he's been in politics or government. What he says therefore about the Bible has at least the authority of long study and usage. In July 2005, speaking at the Baptist World Alliance in Birmingham, England, Mr. Carter noted that there is "one incontrovertible fact" about the relationship between Jesus Christ and women: "he treated them as equal to men," something that was "dramatically different from the prevailing custom of the times." Mr. Carter went on to explain that "although the four Gospels were written by men, they never report an instance of Jesus condoning sexual discrimination or the implied subservience of women. Instead, he deliberately exalted women on many occasions."[1]

I am satisfied that the apostle Paul followed his Lord in this attitude, in spite of many critiques to the contrary. Paul demonstrated once again that the devil is in the details, and that the specifics of any political, sociological, or religious position are often messy. This is especially true when you have to deal with these details in a pagan world—whether it's the pagan world of the first century or the twenty-first. My sympathies are with Paul because he was compelled to be a practical (or if you prefer, a practicing) theologian, rather than a theoretical one. In fact, except perhaps for the epistle to the Romans, Paul never wrote any freestanding theology; rather, his insights and recommendations usually were crafted in the white heat of living issues.

This was especially true in some of the counsel he gave concerning the role of women in home and church. It was no simple matter to define that role for a new culture in the setting of a very old world. Paul could declare boldly that "in Christ Jesus you are all children of God through faith," and that therefore "there is no longer male and female" (Galatians 3:26, 28), but it was terribly complicated to implement such a startling new idea in the perplexing details of a public assembly.

I have come to new sympathy with Paul's problem in the years that I have taught preaching in a theological seminary. I apologize to my women students when I discuss proper pulpit garb. As I've observed it, men and women have a chance of being judged with some fairness in the pulpit as long as they're wearing pulpit robes, but if they choose streetwear, the situation changes. Men enjoy all kinds of latitude (sometimes too much, it seems to me) in what they can wear while ministering at pulpit and altar, but women are open to all kinds of criticism. Not from God, but from human beings whose opinions are shaped largely by the standards of our culture. I tell my women students that this is unfair, but that we have to deal with the way things are, not the way they ought to be. I think perhaps Paul must have felt the same way as he gave counsel regarding female conduct. He was doing the best he could with life as it was lived in the first-century world.

But when Paul is dealing with specific human beings, we see him as the greathearted soul that he was. When at Caesarea he went to the house of Philip, one of the seven original deacons of the early church, Paul obviously had no problem with the fact that Philip's four unmarried daughters "had the gift of prophecy" (Acts 21:8-9), a gift that meant public speaking in the most vigorous and impressive ways. And consider Priscilla and Aquila, wife and husband who like Paul were tentmakers by trade. Paul found such compatibility with them that he not only stayed with them for a time, he had them accompany him to Syria when he went to minister there, and it's clear that they were his aides in ministry. Most of the New Testament references to Priscilla and Aquila place her name first, which suggests that she may well have been a woman of rank and thus given preference to her husband. For Paul, she was a co-worker. Paul gladly worked with women in the ministry of the church, but he had to deal with the same kinds of cultural issues that still pursue us today, and in his attempts to protect the church and its work from unjust criticism, he spelled out details that can sound very offensive to our ears.

But let me get on to a woman named Lydia, because she's the particular person I want to talk about. One of Paul's most exciting places of ministry was Philippi, "a leading city of the district of Macedonia and a Roman colony" (Acts 16:12). This was the Apostle's first venture into Europe, and he chose a strategic city. The Romans had made it such by making it one of their colonies—that is, a city that was an intentional outpost of Rome. The colony was built around a group of army veterans who had fulfilled their service; the colonists who lived in Philippi dressed like Romans, spoke like Romans, and lived like Romans. As William Barclay put it, "Nowhere was there greater pride in Roman citizenship than in these outposts of Rome."[2]

In most places where the apostles went, they sought first to worship and speak in a synagogue, believing rightly that the Jews were more ready than anyone to hear the message of the Messiah. But there was probably no synagogue in Philippi, so on the Sabbath day Paul and Silas went to the other setting where they were most likely to find—as the writer of Acts puts it—"a place of prayer" (Acts 16:13). There they found that a group of women had gathered. This was not therefore a typical synagogue gathering, which would have been made up of men; I venture we can call it simply a body of seekers. They were the God-hungry ones, the people who on the day of worship came to a place removed from the dominating paganism of the city so that they might wait on God. And among them was "a certain woman named Lydia, a worshiper of God," who chose to listen to them (Acts 16:14).

Believe me, there are listeners and there are listeners, and as one who has spent most of my life trying to do business with a variety of listeners, I know the difference. The author of the book of Acts, who was apparently on the scene at the time (he writes in the first-person plural about what "we" were doing), describes Lydia as listening "eagerly to what was said by Paul" (Acts 16:14). I have known people who listen indifferently, cautiously, and half-heartedly; and I've known those who, though present, seem not to be listening at all. I've also known those who listen thoughtfully and inquisitively, both of which hold great promise. But there's nothing quite like the person who listens eagerly. Such a person hears not only what is being said but also, quite often, more than what is actually said. When I see a person listening eagerly, I know that person is probably hearing a better sermon or lesson than I'm delivering.

And in the process, such listeners make preachers or teachers rise above themselves. When I'm on the rostrum or in the pulpit, I look for those eager souls because I know they will invigorate me. The apostle Paul acknowledged to the people in Corinth that he knew they said of him, "His letters are weighty and strong, but his bodily presence is weak, and his speech contemptible" (2 Corinthians 10:10). I submit that Paul rose to new levels of public address with Lydia in the audience. An eager listener can do wonders for an average preacher. Some churches that are looking for a more effective preacher might try putting several eager listeners in the line of sight of the preacher and see what happens. Such listeners can, in a little while, upgrade the quality of the preacher. On the other hand, if the eager listeners lose their eagerness after a month, there may be something seriously wrong with the preacher.

But of course eager listeners can also, in some instances, be superficial listeners. They may be the kind of people Jesus had in mind in his parable of the sower: "They sprang up quickly, since they had no depth of soil" (Matthew 13:5). There are those who are interested in every new thing, and who therefore dispose of any enthusiasm as quickly as a new one comes along. Lydia's eagerness was grounded in depth. Originally from Thyatira, she was almost surely a Gentile who either had become a convert to Judaism or was so attracted to the Jewish truth of one God that she was seeking out Jewish teaching and worship. The writer of Acts describes her simply as "a worshiper of God." In modern parlance that might leave a good deal of latitude; in the language of the book of Acts, I suspect it suggests that she was under at least the broad umbrella of Judaism.

But almost surely she was at the far edges of that umbrella. As an unmarried Gentile woman, she was unable by the laws of Judaism to convert. Obviously she was a convert in her heart, but an outsider by the structures of the institution. This indefinite state in her pilgrimage no doubt helped in her grand step to Christ. Judaism had been a way station for her, a step toward Jesus the Christ. Listening to Paul, who had himself made the journey from Judaism to Christ, she had to feel that at last her journey had its destination. She was baptized, and "her household" with her.

No reference is made to Lydia's husband, so we can conclude that she was either a widow or a divorced or never-married person. Her "household" no doubt refers to her servants and very likely her slaves. Because our culture is so individualistic, we stumble at the concept that when Lydia is converted, her whole household is baptized with her. Were those associated with Lydia required to come along, willy-nilly, with no conversion or conviction of their own? Or was it that her decision was so vigorous and convincing that those closest to her were ready to make the same step? In truth, it's difficult to transpose the setting, the customs, and the thought patterns of the first-century world into our twenty-first-century, Western type of thinking. I venture that where the first-century world—and many of the generations preceding and immediately following—were perhaps unduly communal in their thinking, we are as surely unduly individualistic in ours.

Lydia was a businesswoman. She had to have been a very strong person. Not only was the business world dominated by men but also Lydia had come from another region, which made an extra burden to prove herself. Her business itself, at least within the Jewish community, must have had a marginal position. On the one hand, her product, purple-dye cloth, was very expensive and catered to those who could afford it. But on the other hand, because this dye was extracted from a type of shellfish—a food seen as unclean by the levitical laws—it's quite possible that a person dealing in a shellfish product would also be seen as outside the Jewish laws. This could have added to her impediment in any possible inclusion within Judaism.

Thyatira, from which Lydia came, was a center of the dye industry. Lydia probably immigrated to Philippi to establish a market for her trade there. We have to conclude that she was very successful in her business, since she now had a "household," a body of persons working with and for her, under her direction. And her home was large enough that she could invite Paul and Silas and anyone else traveling with them—certainly including Luke at this time—to have lodging in her home. I repeat that this is a very strong person, one who was able to make her way in a country where she was an alien, in an industry that was both marginal and economically demanding, supervising a contingent of workers—and all the while on a spiritual quest that took precedence over the demands of her daily life. A remarkable human being, by any measure.

With her conversion, Lydia extended herself with what was no doubt a daring act of hospitality: "If you have judged me to be faithful to the Lord, come and stay at my home" (Acts 16:15). Her invitation was no idle formality; as Luke put it, "she prevailed upon us" (16:15). Her "household" now included these preachers whose ministry had so dramatically affected her life. We speak poetically about the "family of God"; Lydia put the idea into action. It was daring to do so. The followers of Jesus represented a small religious movement that was suspect in almost every quarter. It was daring enough just to identify yourself as being sympathetic with such a marginal body; Lydia chose to make her home their headquarters.

Not too long afterward she had reason, if she wanted to, to question the wisdom of her own hospitality. The apostles got in trouble with their preaching and a particular act of deliverance, and Paul and Silas were thrown into prison. Those who saw to their arrest were influential enough to have them put "in the innermost cell," where their feet were fastened in stocks (Acts 16:24). I don't know what Lydia did

113

that night, but based on the character and personality we've already seen in her, I'm confident that she prayed for her two spiritual leaders.

About midnight, not only were Paul and Silas miraculously delivered from prison but also the jailer and his household were converted. The next morning the public officials apologized to the apostles for their irregular arrest. So as soon as they left the prison, Paul and Silas and the rest of their company "went to Lydia's home," where they met with "the brothers and sisters" who had gathered there, and "encouraged" them (Acts 16:40). Quite clearly, Lydia's home had become the ex officio headquarters for the new Christian body in Philippi. To speak of the church at Philippi was to speak of Lydia. And of course Paul and Silas went there, not simply because it was "headquarters" but because it was the best place to go for renewal after the trying experience of arrest, scourging, and restoration. At such a time, we want to be with someone of spiritual strength. Lydia was already such a person.

This remarkable businesswoman has a unique place in the history of the church. She is the first-named Christian in Europe. As we have noted, she was not a European by birth, but she had made her home in Philippi, had established a business there, and had become part of a small community of seekers after God. God honored her hunger, and in the providence of a meeting one Sabbath day, she heard the good news of new life in Jesus Christ, and with eagerness she bought it. Still today if you visit that area, you will find that the springs near a gate called the Krenides is referred to as "Lydia's River," the place, tradition says, where she was baptized.

Readers whose ethnic roots are European may want to claim Lydia as their special spiritual ancestor, since she was the first declared follower of Christ on European soil. And businesswomen may feel close to her because she is "their kind of person"—someone who was bright, articulate, aggressive, and hungry for God.

But all of us who love Christ wish that we might more surely emulate this woman who one day laid aside her many pressing concerns in order to care for her eternal soul. And because of that day, there's a riverbank outside Philippi that still bears Lydia's name. And many of us, whatever our ethnic roots, whatever our careers, would like to claim her as our spiritual kin.

CHAPTER ELEVEN

Mary in Life
and Legend

Scripture Reading: Luke 1:46-55

It is sometimes said that men have written history, and therefore women haven't gotten their fair share of the pages. In spite of that, it's surprising how many notable women come to mind as one skips over the top of history. We immediately think of Deborah, an early judge of Israel; Cleopatra, one of the most powerful leaders of the ancient world during her time as queen of Egypt; Elizabeth I and Victoria, queens of England; Teresa of Avila, who established

seventeen monastic houses and left us with devotional literature that is still sought out today; Frances Willard, a person
of so many achievements in so many areas that when she
died, flags were lowered in both Washington, D.C., and in
Chicago her adopted city, and 30,000 people filed through
Chicago's Willard Hall on a cold February day in order to
pay honor at her death;[1] and Marie Curie, who won Nobel
Prizes in both physics and chemistry. One thinks too of
Eleanor Roosevelt, whose work in drawing attention to the
needs of the poor and of the racially segregated may have
made as much of a long-range impact on history as the
achievements of her president-husband, Franklin Delano
Roosevelt, in leading America through depression and war.
Most recently, Mother Teresa was perhaps the best-known
personality in the world through some years of the late twentieth century.

But after all that recitation, I dare still to say that no
one—absolutely no one—has attained a place in history and
surely in public affection to compare with Mary the mother
of Jesus. Millions recite her name in prayer every day.
Thousands of institutions, in every part of the world, carry
her name, institutions as diverse as elementary schools, col-
leges and universities, hospitals, homes for orphans and the
aged, and of course churches. But even more compelling is
the affection—yes, even adoration—in which Mary is held by
millions. Some of the poorest and most depressed persons in
the world think of her as their closest friend; they somehow

find particular strength and comfort in approaching God under the embrace of her name.

So who was she? The Bible tells her story in its straightforward way, with little adornment; we have to turn to novelists, poets, composers, and moviemakers for the embellishments her story seems to demand. When the angel Gabriel was sent by God to speak to Mary he went to "a town in Galilee called Nazareth, to a virgin engaged to a man whose name was Joseph, of the house of David" (Luke 1:26-27). And Luke continues, in what seems almost an afterthought, "The virgin's name was Mary" (1:27). I think I can say, without fear of contradiction, that her name continues to be the most popular woman's name in much, if not all, of the Western world—because in addition to those millions who have the name "Mary," there are the additional millions who carry one of the more than sixty-five derivative names, such as Marie, Marsha, Marilyn, Marian, and Marianne.

When the angel visited Mary, we can judge that she was probably—based on the patterns of the world in which she lived—no more than fifteen years old. Before her trip to Bethlehem I doubt that she had ever traveled any farther than to Jerusalem, the kind of journey devout Jews made for the holy feast days. Was she a beautiful girl? Of course we like to think so, because we build romantic legends around her. It's altogether possible, however, that if we had lived in her village twenty centuries ago, we wouldn't have noticed her beyond any of the other teenage girls in Nazareth.

119

She grew up in a way of life that was simple beyond our imagining. In truth, the women of thousands of villages in Africa, Asia, and the Middle East would find it easier to picture Mary's way of life than you and I are likely to do. Hers was a world in which people spent most of their time simply keeping alive; the basic maintenance of life, that we dispose of now via our mechanical contraptions, was for Mary and her friends essentially the whole of life. There weren't many excitements to add variety to her days; life itself was excitement enough: the freshness of each new day, the warmth of family, the naturalness of friendship that marked village life, and in time the prospect of love, marriage, and children; these were enough. Perhaps we should envy Mary the ability to find fullness in life itself without undue dependence on the externals that probably do more, at times, to distract us from living than to enrich life.

Well, the time came when Mary got excitement. Again, Luke's account seems so unembellished that we want terribly to add to it. How would you feel if an angel appeared suddenly with the announcement, "Greetings, favored one! The Lord is with you" (Luke 1:28)? You know what? I don't think Mary was as startled by this greeting as you and I would be. The Bible says that "she was much perplexed by his words and pondered what sort of greeting this might be" (Luke 1:29), but it doesn't indicate that the holy visitor himself upset her. Why not? Probably because she lived in a more spiritual world than you and I ordinarily do. She and her contemporaries expected that God might visit their lives in order to accomplish some divine purpose. By unfortunate contrast, we are so absorbed with the immediate that we are hardly open to the transcendent. And that's our poverty. At best, Mary probably had one pair of sandals, but she had a great deal of soul. She wouldn't have rated a page in a fashion magazine, but if we could have spent an hour with her it's quite likely we would have gone away feeling that our fascination with fashion is embarrassingly trivial.

Mary has left us with a song that is known around the world as the *Magnificat*, her cry of praise to God for the trust placed in her. In it she acknowledges the "lowliness" of her state, but she goes on quite artlessly to say, "Surely, from now on all / generations will call me / blessed" (Luke 1:48). The artlessness is for a reason; she knows that the honor paid to her is not of her doing: "for the Mighty One has done / great things for me, / and holy is his name" (Luke 1:49).

Mary won her revered place in the world by being a mother, the mother of Jesus of Nazareth. Catholics refer to her as "the Mother of God," in respect for our creedal confession that Jesus Christ is "God from God, Light from Light, true God from true God."[2] A cynic or a tough-minded critic might say that simply being a mother is hardly enough to merit her extraordinary place of honor and adoration; after all, literally billions of women, the vast majority without even passing recognition, have borne children into the world. Yet Mary's role is singular.

121

The biblical account of her life is presented in a total of only a few hundred words. After the birth of Jesus and the journey to Egypt and then to Nazareth, we have only one reference in a period of some thirty years. The story refers to the time when the family makes a traditional religious pilgrimage to Jerusalem, during which Jesus, a boy of twelve by this time, engages in a remarkable discussion with some religious leaders. (See Luke 2:41-52.) After that, Mary reappears only a few times during the ministry of Jesus, and with particular poignancy at the time of his crucifixion. When the book of Acts sets the stage for the birth of the church on the day of Pentecost, it lists the most significant persons present at the time, naming the eleven remaining apostles, and then: "All these were constantly devoting themselves to prayer, together with certain women, *including Mary the mother of Jesus* [italics mine], as well as his brothers" (Acts 1:14). Reflecting on Mary's presence in that setting, one writer has suggested that just as, in Bethlehem, she had cared for the infant Jesus, now, in Jerusalem, she was nurturing the infant church.

The reference in the opening chapter of Acts is the last time Mary is mentioned in the story of the church, but there's no doubt about the importance she had from the beginning in the preaching of the first Christians. When Matthew's Gospel was written (probably around A.D. 70), the author not only makes Mary the key figure in the birth of Jesus but also identifies her with the prophecies of Isaiah six centuries earlier: "All this took place to fulfill what had been spoken

by the Lord through the prophet: 'Look, the virgin shall conceive and bear a son, / and they shall name him Emmanuel,'
/ which means, 'God is with us' " (Matthew 1:22-23; see also
Isaiah 7:14). The earliest Christian theologians—including
Jerome, Justin Martyr, Tertullian, Chrysostom, and
Augustine—preached and wrote upon this theme. Mary's
crucial place was therefore established not only in the beauty and sentiment of the Christmas story and in the life of
Jesus but also in the basic theology of the Christian faith. No
wonder, then, that when the faith is summarized in the powerful language of the Apostles' Creed, we have specific reference to Mary: "he [Jesus] was born of the virgin Mary."

All of the apostles and several other biblical personalities
soon became part of legend and myth in the early centuries
of the church, but no one more than the Virgin Mary. She
caught the fancy of early believers in a measure beyond anyone else. One doesn't need to be much of a theologian to realize why this would be true, nor does one need to have much
imagination. Mary's role in the story is unique, so of course
she is crucial to our theology. But for all kinds of human reasons she also appeals to our imaginations and our emotions.
No wonder, then, that legends were built around her.

Do these legends matter, beyond idle curiosity? I believe
so. As I have said in another book and context, Phyllis
McGinley, the Pulitzer Prize–winning poet, had it right when
she said in *Saint Watching*, "Behind every myth lies a truth,
behind every legend is reality."[3] I suspect that in a great many

instances—perhaps in most—the legends around Mary and other biblical figures have their origins in true happenings.

Some who read Mary's story will feel uncomfortable with the acclaim poured upon her, especially when the praise seems to lift Mary to divinity. Others will find the language associated with Mary florid and unduly sentimental. Still others will be troubled by doctrinal issues, in that some of the teachings regarding Mary seem to Protestant eyes to be without biblical foundation or even contrary to biblical teaching. In each case, I urge that we suspend some of our usual patterns of judgment, and try to understand why Mary the Mother of Jesus has attained such a unique place in our human story.

As I have already indicated, the Bible actually tells us very little about Mary. Perhaps it is partly this scarcity of data that has evoked the wealth of myth and legend, as if fascinated and adoring folk felt there surely had to be more to the story than the few pages given in the Scriptures. But Martin Luther gave a straightforward answer to any question about the Bible's limited references to Mary when he wrote that the Gospels had said enough when they called Mary the Mother of Jesus—and eight times at that. We can give her no greater title, although creative worshipers have tried to do so; nor can we put together any stories that give Mary greater stature than that which she earned by her care of Jesus from birth to Calvary. Some of the earnest miracle stories attached to her seem trivial and distracting compared with the simple account of a woman who, as she watched her boy grow, "treasured all these things in her heart" (Luke 2:51).

The great second-century theologian Irenaeus taught that just as Eve while yet a virgin disobeyed and became the cause of death, so Mary as a virgin obeyed and became God's instrument of salvation. As early as the fourth century, some prayed to the Virgin Mary, notably Ephraim the Syrian and Gregory of Nazianzus. Probably in the fifth century, the empress Eudoxia built a church at the place where tradition said Mary was born, and where presumably her parents lived in their last years. It was also in the fifth century that the tradition became established that Mary had died in Jerusalem and had been buried in Gethsemane. The common view, especially in the Catholic tradition, is that she died of love, that her desire to be with her Son brought a dissolving of the ties of body and soul. This thought has been common since the Middle Ages.

Two Catholic dogmas concerning Mary have been declared by papal decree. In 1854 Pope Pius IX issued the doctrine of the Immaculate Conception—that is, that Mary was conceived "without the stain of original sin," with a soul created in pure holiness and innocence. In 1950 Pope Pius XII proclaimed the Assumption of the Virgin Mary as an element of Catholic doctrine. This doctrine teaches that at the end of her life Mary was taken "body and soul" into heaven by angels. Catholics celebrate the Feast of the Assumption

125

each year on August 15. These two teachings, which are very dear to many Catholics, are often seen as a major point of disagreement with most Protestants.

I speak of course as a Protestant when I say that I see no need of the two doctrines I have just mentioned. But I say this out of no disparaging of Mary the Mother of Jesus. I am simply saying that these doctrines are not needed to bring honor to Mary. If God chose her to be the instrument by which Jesus Christ came into our world, nothing that can be said beyond that can add to her significance, her holy beauty, and her singular place in the kingdom of heaven. Mary's person is such that any attempt to expand upon that significance is like seeking to add a few more dabs of paint to a masterpiece. A masterpiece is complete in itself, and anything added to it is a distraction rather than a benefit.

The angel told Mary she was "favored of God." Each of us who claims Christ as Lord is thankful to God that this is so. We are grateful that a Jewish girl in a quiet Galilean village answered, "Here am I, the servant of the Lord; let it be with me according to your word" (Luke 1:38).

CHAPTER TWELVE

Why Mary?

Scripture Reading: Luke 1:26-38

So after reading even a brief summary of the biblical story of Mary the Mother of Jesus and the aura that has grown around her through the centuries, most of us are likely to be left with a question: Why Mary? Of all the young women in the Middle East at that time—or to put the challenge even more broadly, of all the women in human history—how is it that this Palestinian teenager has come to be revered throughout the world? Or how is it that God chose her for such a singular role?

As you can see, this is my starting point, that Mary was chosen. I don't think she simply grew into her role—though

I'm very sure she grew with it. If you believe (as I do) that God cares about our planet and its inhabitants, then you believe that God is involved in our history, and that at times God even chooses to intervene in its unfolding. Furthermore, both logic and observation convince most of us that God makes these interventions via human beings. God has the right, being God, to do business in our planet by any means available—and for God, the possibilities would seem infinite. But from what I can observe, God usually has chosen to work through the fallible and exciting lives of humans. Other ways might be tidier, but I'm glad God chose us humans as the usual vehicles of action, since I myself belong to that erratic body.

At the same time, however, I dare to think that God's choices are logical. Mind you, we don't always see the logic, sometimes not even when we are part of the operation. But I think there's nothing random about God's actions. The Scriptures portray a God who plans ahead and who seems never to be caught off guard. Personally, I think it is possible for even those who are *called* to not recognize God's purposes or to frustrate those purposes by untoward actions or stupid responses; but when we do, God takes the flawed stuff we contribute and manages still to bring forth a finished product.

Sometimes God starts early. When Jeremiah received his call, it was with the compelling word, "Before I formed you in the womb I knew you, and before you were born I conse-

crated you; I appointed you a prophet to the nations"
(Jeremiah 1:5). It was good of God to apprise Jeremiah of
such long-range expectations, because certainly there were
times when Jeremiah needed all the help he could get. In the
same fashion, a psalmist felt his calling so strongly that he
wrote, "In your book were written all the days that were
formed for me, when none of them as yet existed" (Psalm
139:16).

So why did God choose a Jeremiah, a Saul of Tarsus, a
David? And most especially, why did God choose Mary? If
some of these persons were, like Jeremiah, chosen even
before they were born, on what grounds were the choices
made? Did God choose them on the basis of their genetic
code? If one believes that God is the ultimate Creator, including the source of our mysterious genetic formations, it isn't
unreasonable to think that God works with such data—and
indeed, that because we are still free moral agents in what we
do with our genetic inclinations, the active choices remain in
our hands even after God calls us. As a person's life proceeds
to unfold, we can try to imagine what God saw in that particular individual to make him or her seem a special choice,
and sometimes the answer is hard to come by.

In Mary's case it's clear from the beginning that God
was dealing with real human stuff. There's a tendency with
some in the Roman Catholic tradition—and among some
Protestants too—to romanticize Mary to a point where she
hardly seems real. The Bible doesn't do this. When Mary first

STRONG WAS HER FAITH

enters the story in Luke's Gospel, she is "a virgin engaged to a man whose name was Joseph, of the house of David" (Luke 1:27). She is living an ordinary life in a Galilean village and, like any other girl in that village, is anticipating marriage. Some traditions have insisted that she had already pledged herself to perpetual virginity, but to take such a position one has to attribute some deceit to Mary in her making a betrothal and wedding contract. On the contrary, it is clear that she was a girl who lived with the same dreams, fears, and longings of any young woman of her age and time.

Was she more sensitive to God than young women in general? I think so. I believe that God works with all kinds of humans, but that God does the best work with those who have a disposition toward heaven's goals. When the angel said, "Greetings, favored one! The Lord is with you" (Luke 1:28), Mary didn't respond with the fear that marks the objects of so many other angelic visitations; the writer says simply that "she was much perplexed by his words and pondered what sort of greeting this might be" (Luke 1:29). That is, she chose not to draw back from the visitor or to argue with the call, but to enter into a wrestling in her own soul as to why God had chosen her. And more important, she entered into this wrestling on God's side. That is, she did not, like Moses or Gideon, try to convince God to look elsewhere. Instead, she *pondered* what God might have in mind—with the obvious conclusion that she intended to cooperate with those purposes once she was clear about them.

But as soon as the angel visit was complete, Mary did a human thing. A wise thing, mind you, but a very human one. She went to a trusted older relative in whom she had seen (as so many had) the grace and goodness that demonstrated true godliness. It's interesting that she didn't go to her mother. This is not to say that her mother was not a good person, but it may suggest that Mary sensed—as a wise young person might—that her mother was too emotionally involved in Mary's life to be able to counsel her effectively at such a peculiar and frightening juncture. And she stayed with her cousin Elizabeth three months, probably almost to the point of Elizabeth's delivery of her own son.

Mary's setting at the time of Jesus' birth was unconventional and challenging. Forced by a government decree to travel for several difficult days from Nazareth to Bethlehem for the purpose of a census, she and Joseph arrived for the baby's birth but not in time to get satisfactory lodging. From a human point of view Mary came from hardy enough stock and lived in a culture accustomed enough to pain that she was ready to deliver her baby even though the circumstances were unfavorable. The biblical writers offer no commentary on her experience; we don't know the extent of her pain or if she had to deal with extraordinary issues. No doubt some legends suggest that she was spared the usual pains of childbirth, perhaps on the ground that those pains were associated with Eve's original sin. But nothing in the Scriptures suggests such an understanding.

But Mary had other pains that were unique to her role. God's callings are wonderful, but sometimes they are also lonely. The greater one's sense of purpose, the greater also the possibility of question and depression. When Jesus was still an infant, the family left by night to escape King Herod's wrath. Mary may well have wondered during that trip if bearing God's Son would mean nothing but long, emotionally perilous journeys: Nazareth to Bethlehem, Bethlehem to Egypt, and what next? She must often have pondered how God's plan could possibly play out through a couple as humbly equipped as she and Joseph were. Still and all, however, Mary was a product of a faith people. She had grown up with the stories of Abraham and Sarah, the songs of David, and the weekly miracle of the Sabbath. God had preserved her people through the slavery of Egypt, the failures of judges and kings, the invasions of enemy nations, and persecutions that would have wiped out any ordinary nation; yet here they were, still expecting the purposes of God to be fulfilled through them. With such a heritage and with her unique sense of purpose, Mary would survive.

When Jesus was twelve, Mary had an experience that was little less than a renewal of her call. The family had gone to Jerusalem for the Passover festival. In that world of extended families, Joseph and Mary thought nothing of it when Jesus was not with them at the beginning of their return; it was as natural for him to be with other villagers in their group of travelers as to be with them. But when Jesus was not with them at the end of the first day, fear set in. They returned to Jerusalem to seek him out, and found him at last—of all things!—"in the temple, sitting among the teachers, listening to them and asking them questions" (Luke 2:46). And if Mary and Joseph were surprised to find him there, they had to be still more surprised by the respect the nation's finest rabbis were showing their son.

But Mary was a mother first and a theologian second. Her first comment was a thoroughly maternal one: "Child, why have you treated us like this?" (Luke 2:48). She was speaking the sentence all of us have heard our parents say, and that some of us have said to children of our own: "Do you realize how you've made us worry?" Jesus' reply seems almost casual: He was where they should have expected him to be, "in my Father's house." Luke says that "they did not understand what he said to them," but that Jesus went with them back to Nazareth where he "was obedient to them." Then, this telling sentence: "His mother treasured all these things in her heart" (Luke 2:49-51). I see something artful in the way Luke reports the incident; he does not say, "*Mary* treasured all these things," but "*His mother*." Jesus is the center of the story.

I wonder how Mary treasured these things in her heart during the next thirty years? We humans want our promises fulfilled as quickly as possible. Instead, Mary watched her boy become a man under altogether ordinary circumstances. We have no reliable evidence that Jesus enjoyed any special position or respect in their village; indeed, it seems that when he came back after attaining some recognition elsewhere as a teacher, his fellow villagers were rather mystified by his success. We assume that Joseph died at some point in Jesus' young manhood, and that Jesus took up the responsibility for the household.

So it's easy to imagine Mary falling asleep, night after night, year after year, wondering about the remarkable experiences of so long ago: the visit from the angel Gabriel; then the dramatic words from her cousin Elizabeth; the visit by shepherds and wise men; the heralding by Simeon and Anna when she and Joseph had presented Jesus at the temple; and of course, that peculiar incident when Jesus was twelve. But what did it all mean now, when every day for her son was that of a village carpenter—with his measuring, building, joshing with neighbors, laughing with the village men, settling prices for building projects—what had happened to the dreams of those years so long past?

Then one day Jesus said it was time for him to leave and to begin teaching. I wonder if Mary played a counseling role at this point. I think of what happened early in Jesus' ministry, when he and his disciples attended a wedding where Mary was present (John 2:1-11). When the family ran out of wine, Mary reported it to Jesus with the implied question, "What are you going to do about this?" Jesus answered, "My hour has not yet come," but his mother would have nothing to do with such a statement. She instructed the servants to follow his orders, as if she hadn't heard a word her son had said. Mary seemed to sense her son's hour when he was still cautious. Here is one of the moments when we see something of the quality that would have caused God to call her.

But there were also times of another nature. As Jesus' ministry developed, something happened within the Nazareth family. When Jesus returned to Nazareth soon after appointing his twelve apostles, crowds gathered around to see him, in numbers so great "that they [Jesus and the apostles] could not even eat" (Mark 3:20). "When [Jesus'] family heard it, they went out to restrain him, for people were saying, 'He has gone out of his mind'" (Mark 3:21, adapted). Was Mary part of the family in their fear that Jesus had "gone out of his mind"? We know only that "then his mother and his brothers came; and standing outside, they sent to him and called him" (Mark 3:31), apparently on their mission to "restrain him." When Jesus was told that his mother and brothers and sisters were outside, he said to those who were listening to his teaching, "Here are my mother and my brothers! Whoever does the will of God is my brother and sister and mother" (Mark 3:34-35).

Was Mary acting in unbelief when she came with other family members to talk with Jesus? We can't say. Perhaps Mary hoped to be a moderating voice in the proposed discussion between the brothers and Jesus. Mothers, by long practice, can be good at that sort of thing. Or perhaps she had herself begun to wonder. Caught in the struggles of competing arguments and incipient loyalties, the human soul can swing like a pendulum, first one way and then another, sometimes unreasonably far to right or left, but always propelled by forces seen and unseen. In my opinion—one set in the conviction that Mary was human and therefore susceptible to the struggles all of us have to deal with—she may have been balancing in her soul the experiences that she had for so long "treasured in her heart" with these frightening new developments.

This in no way diminishes Mary or impugns her grand faith and loyalty. Faith and loyalty that are not at some point thrust into the cauldron of testing really have very little meaning. If she wavered at this moment between the appeals of her other children and the uniqueness she saw in this son who was now embarked on a course that made her feel almost a stranger—well, I can only hurt with her pain.

I suspect that Mary's emotions went into roller-coaster mode as Jesus' ministry moved to its climax. There was that ecstatic hour on the day we now call Palm Sunday, when it looked as if at any moment Jesus might set up his kingdom. Even the power of Rome could have seemed pregnable at that moment. But darkness began to settle in a few days later; mother that she was, Mary must have sensed the mounting anguish in Jesus' soul, while others were busy arguing about who would be greatest among them when Jesus took the throne.

Then there was the terrifying night of Jesus' arrest, followed by the mockery of a trial, the public scourging and humiliation, and at last the crucifixion. Most of the people who came close to the cross in the final hours were those who wanted to mock Jesus; only a few of his once devoted followers were within painful reach. But of course Mary was there, along with her sister and Mary Magdalene—and yes, that disciple who is identified in John's Gospel as "the disciple whom [Jesus] loved" (John 19:26, adapted). Somehow during the hours when each breath was a struggle, with the limitations of the body and the ravages of hell, Jesus spoke a special, last, caring word to his mother: "Woman, here is your son." Then, to the disciple standing close by, Jesus said of Mary, "Here is your mother." The Gospel writer reports that "from that hour the disciple took her into his own home" (John 19:26-27).

As Joseph of Arimathea took Jesus' body for burial, Mary could think of the day some thirty-three years earlier when the angel told her she was a "favored one," and wonder what kind of favor it had been. She had enjoyed all the joys of motherhood, but she had suffered pain too. Simeon had told her it would be so, when he appeared suddenly at Jesus' service of purification. He had prophesied the glory this life would bring, but then had appended a somber note: "and a sword will pierce your own soul too" (Luke 2:35). Mary didn't know at the time what that meant, but she felt the inescapable truth of what the old man was saying. But now, at this moment, she must have smiled woefully as she whispered to herself, "He didn't tell me how severe that sword would be." And here at the Crucifixion was perhaps the worst of all, to see her baby violated, humiliated, brutalized.

But I believe she was at peace. The writer of the letter to the Hebrews would say of the Hebrew saints that they all died without having received what was promised (see Hebrews 11:39). But Mary did. She saw the promise written in the blood of her son. She could walk from this place of death not really alone, not the least afraid, and utterly confident of the purposes of God. She had finished the work she had been given to do.

I believe in God's logic. And God's logical choice? Mary, the Nazareth girl who skipped along with playmates, who took her turn each day going to the village well on her family's behalf, who entered into betrothal and childbirth and marriage; God chose well. Our human history in general, and our planet's faith history in particular, are crowded with great human beings, particularly with women who have done nobly. But Mary, Mother of Jesus, is quite surely in a class by herself. God chose her for a role like no other. And God chose well.

Suggestions for Leading a Study of *Strong Was Her Faith*

Shannon Sumrall

This study guide is designed to enhance your experience of *Strong Was Her Faith: Women of the New Testament*, by J. Ellsworth Kalas, by assisting you in your reflection and discussion of the book. The study guide is grouped into sections by chapter. In each chapter section you will find a brief summary of the chapter, followed by reflection / discussion questions, and a prayer focus pertaining to that particular woman of faith.

The reflection/discussion questions will guide you in examining the lives of these women of the New Testament and the way their characteristics are embodied in the women around us. Women are relational beings, and these questions are designed both to help us remember women who have blessed us in relationship, and inspire us to bless others in relationship with the Lord.

The prayer focus sections include prayers of petition or thanksgiving to the Lord, as well as interactive prayer activities. Colossians 4:2 reads, "Devote yourselves to prayer, keeping alert in it with thanksgiving." In this context, our whole lives can be an opportunity for prayer. A conversation, a move to action, an artistic creation, a remembrance, a word of praise, and testimony of a life lived well—all can constitute prayer. It is also important to note that our prayers can be offered both with others and alone.

The hope is that the materials offered in this study guide, together with your own reflection and insights from your reading, will be a reminder that we are all needed in the body of Christ. As Ephesians 4:11-13 tells us:

> The gifts he gave were that some would be apostles, some prophets, some evangelists, some pastors and teachers, to equip the saints for the work of ministry, for building up the body of Christ, until all of us come to the unity of the faith and of the knowledge of the Son of God, to maturity, to the measure of the full stature of Christ.

140

Suggestions for Group Study Leaders

Remember that every group is unique. Talk with the members of your group to determine a pace and an approach to reading and study that feels comfortable and appropriate for all. Give yourself permission to modify and adapt the format of this study as it suits your group's needs.

Help ensure that your group will be a safe place to share personal ideas. Emphasize the importance of mutual respect and confidentiality. Let all group members have an equal opportunity to participate. Look for ways to involve everyone, while at the same time respecting the fact that each person has a different comfort zone.

Allowing time during your group meeting to share prayer requests and to pray for and with one another can be a valuable part of the study and may help you bring it from the "head" level to the "heart" level. Providing food and beverages as snacks or as a meal can be an asset to fellowship, and designating a certain week when the group engages in a special planned activity together may provide an opportunity for fellowship and spiritual growth as well. Encourage group members to interact with the chapter material through activities such as independent research, journaling, painting, creating a collage, or online dialogue before your group comes together each week. These sorts of activities can be shared among group members or may be done individually as a means of personal growth and reflection.

Above all, sit and listen for the Lord's direction. God will lead and guide you and your group, perhaps in ways that are unexpected. Enjoy the journey!

Suggestions for Participants

Remember that you bring a unique perspective and experience, and your group would not be complete without your presence. Remember to read through the chapter material before the group meeting and look for ways to interact with it. This can be done through independent research, journaling, online dialogue, creating original works of art, and many other ways. The important thing is to record your thoughts and to interact with the subject matter. In addition to your own learning, this kind of interactive study can help you bring a greater depth to the group experience.

If you do not have an opportunity to read the chapter material before your meeting, there are still ways to be involved and to share in the journey with others. The prayer is that through this study you will find yourself closer to the heart of the Lord and to being the person God has made you to be. This study is a celebration of women of the New Testament, as well as the women of today. May it be a joyful journey!

Chapter 1
Elizabeth: A Friend in Need

Chapter Summary

This chapter focuses on Elizabeth, the mother of John the Baptist and a cousin to Mary, who provided a Christlike and selfless response to Mary's arrival at a time in her life when being self-absorbed might have been not only excused but perhaps even expected.

Reflection / Discussion Questions

1. How does the old saying "the apple doesn't fall far from the tree" seem to be applicable to Elizabeth?

2. What were the repercussions in the ancient Near East of being childless in marriage?

3. What was Elizabeth's response to being childless?

4. How could Elizabeth's response help prepare her for what the coming years would bring?

5. Revelation 3:20 says that God is standing and knocking at the door of our hearts, waiting for us to open the door. What can we surmise about Elizabeth's character that caused her to hold open the door for the infilling of the Holy Spirit?

6. Elizabeth's tender response to the Lord allowed her to be sensitive to the Spirit and also to Mary's situation. How can we position our hearts so that we will be able to respond tenderly to the Lord and to our brothers and sisters in need as well?

7. How was Elizabeth's response to Mary reflected in the witness of John the Baptist during the final years of his ministry?

8. For Elizabeth and Zechariah, it may have seemed as though their being childless was a punishment, when instead it might be said that God had a perfect plan for Jesus and

John to be born around the same time. In what circumstance in your life might there be a bigger plan than you can see right now?

9. Do you recall a specific time when you have needed an Elizabeth to help carry you? What was it about this person that allowed you to know it was safe to be with her in your time of need?

10. When have you had a friend in need and provided your presence? What gifts or qualities were you able to use so that your friend felt safe to come to you?

11. How have your reading, reflection, and discussion of chapter 1 helped or challenged you? What other important points or questions from this chapter would you like to explore?

Prayer Focus

Sit with God, and ask God to work in and through you to help you get closer to making "utterly unselfish steps of discipleship."

Again and again throughout Scripture, we as God's people are admonished to remember. Remembering stirs up gratitude, which leads to praise and draws us back to the Lord. Think of a person in your life who has been an Elizabeth for you at a particularly difficult time and remember her. If possible, share with this person your gratitude for her, or share with another person in your life about the experience.

All good gifts are from you, God. Thank you for friends like Elizabeth who journey with us. Help us be that kind of friend as well. Amen.

Chapter 2
Anna: She Knew How to Wait

Chapter Summary

This chapter focuses on Anna, a woman whose persistence in prayer and waiting on the Lord gave her the opportunity to recognize Jesus for who he was and to welcome him to the world.

Reflection / Discussion Questions

1. Though Anna's tribe was from a different region, what might have brought them to Jerusalem?

2. As a female in the ancient Near East, what was significant about the gifting that Anna had been blessed with?

3. What was Anna's main occupation? How might she have supported herself?

4. We are told that Anna waited in the Temple, in fasting and in prayer, for well over sixty years. What do you believe kept her hope alive as she waited?

5. What is your explanation for Anna's recognition of the infant Jesus?

6. As the author points out, Anna delivered the news of Jesus Christ to a specific group, with whom she had been waiting. What is the significance of waiting on the Lord with others?

7. What is your understanding of fasting and its part in the Christian life?

8. Share your recollection of a woman in your life who has "waited well" among extremely difficult circumstances. Make an effort to express gratitude for her this week.

9. On what are you waiting at this point in your life?

10. What can help sustain you in your time of waiting?

11. How have your reading, reflection, and discussion of chapter 2 helped or challenged you? What other important points or questions from this chapter would you like to explore?

Prayer Focus

Anna was called to wait on the Lord and to pray as the major focus of life. Could this way of life be a calling for you? Do you know someone whose heart seems to beat in time with this calling? Ask someone in your circle or group to pray with you about this calling, and what it may look like in your life if it is in fact part of your design.

If you never have fasted before, give some thought to discussing this practice with a spiritual advisor or pastor. There are many excellent resources on the discipline of fasting and how to begin if you feel so led.

Dear God, thank you that when you call us to wait and pray, you do show up and let us catch a glimpse of you. That is truly amazing!

Chapter 3
Martha, the Disciplined

Chapter Summary

This chapter focuses on Martha, whose discipline and hospitality became an avenue for growth and for experiencing the Lord's grace and mercy.

Reflection / Discussion Questions

1. How has Martha been remembered throughout history?

2. What miraculous event was Martha privy to? How do you think that may have changed how she lived her life?

3. What strengths did Martha possess?

4. How was Martha's greatest gift a hindrance to her time with Jesus?

5. What would you consider your greatest spiritual gift(s)? Do your gifts point you toward spending time with Jesus, or are they a hindrance at times? Explain.

6. How can you remind yourself to focus on Jesus rather than simply focusing on your spiritual gifts themselves?

7. Jesus "corrected" Martha, and though she could have responded in a variety of ways, she chose to continue following him. How do you think you would respond if Jesus brought a correction for you?

8. Can hospitality be a form of worship? Why or why not?

9. Recall and share something about a woman in your life who has opened her home and showered others with hospitality.

10. What area of hospitality is God calling you to at this time in your life?

11. How have your reading, reflection, and discussion of chapter 3 helped or challenged you? What other important points or questions from this chapter would you like to explore?

Prayer Focus

When Martha was upset about her situation, she chose to take her frustration to Jesus. Think of an area in your life where you need to bring your frustration to Jesus and to listen for his response as you bring it before him; the response may not be what you expect, but it might draw you deeper into relationship with him.

Dear Lord, you see us in the midst of our trying to get it right, and you love us even when we fail miserably. Help us to be teachable in response to correction so that we too may declare who you are.

Chapter 4
Mary, the Extravagant

Chapter Summary

This chapter focuses on Mary, whose love was absolutely uncontained and who poured out herself at the feet of Jesus Christ.

Reflection / Discussion Questions

1. What might have spurred Mary's act of anointing Jesus and wiping his feet?

2. Did the disciples who were criticizing Mary's action have a valid point? Why or why not? Was the cost of the perfume Mary used the real issue? Explain.

3. Why might those around Mary have been uncomfortable with her unashamed outpouring of love?

4. What does extravagance look like for us today?

5. What did the author mean when he said that Mary's gift was "on time"?

6. If possible, reflect on and share an example of a woman who has loved extravagantly in your life. How will you remember her today?

7. How might God be calling you to be extravagant?

8. The author compared Mary's extravagance with that of God. How has God loved us extravagantly?

9. In the act of anointing Jesus' feet, Mary gave the gift of herself. When did you give Jesus, or how might you give him, the gift of yourself?

10. Mary is remembered for her act of devotion. What act would you like to be remembered for?

11. How have your reading, reflection, and discussion of chapter 4 helped or challenged you? What other important points or questions from this chapter would you like to explore?

Prayer Focus

If possible, talk this week with a woman in your life who has loved extravagantly, and discover what the source of love has been for her.

It is so easy to get caught up in the *things* that we have to offer that we forget, or may have never known, that what God wants most is for us to give *ourselves*. Ask God to show you ways in which you may give to God and to others the gift of yourself.

Thank you, Lord, that you are never offended when we pour out extravagant devotion. Help us be unashamed in our time with you.

Chapter 5
The Mighty Widow

Chapter Summary

This chapter focuses on the Mighty Widow, who, though perhaps invisible in her culture, caught the eyes and heart of Jesus Christ.

Reflection / Discussion Questions

1. Where does the story of the Mighty Widow fit in the story of Jesus?

2. Why did the gift of this widow merit attention?

3. What was the widow's motivation? What was her reward for giving all that she had that day?

4. What is it about humanity that allows us to be so awed by the *amount* of a gift that we forget what is *behind* it?

5. What do you see as the major principle in this story?

6. What does *giving* look like to you, and how do you make that determination?

7. How do you reconcile saving for the future with being mighty for the Lord today?

8. Does giving have to be given to the church to "count" for the Lord? If not, what are other options?

9. How can we instill the idea of sacrificial giving into the upcoming generation?

10. Can you recall the story of a woman whose tremendous sacrifice blessed you and allowed you to move forward in giving? If so, how can you honor her today?

11. How have your reading, reflection, and discussion of chapter 5 helped or challenged you? What other important points or questions from this chapter would you like to explore?

Prayer Focus

Talk with someone you know to be a mighty giver, and reflect on this person's experience of giving.

Ask God the question, "How can I be mighty for you?" Whatever "mighty" looks like for you, go for it. It does not have to be neat and tidy—just from your heart. If you aren't sure just yet, wait for a while. The Lord will show you an opportunity to give.

Thank you, Lord, that you do not look at the amount of our giving, but at the heart behind it. Help us to give in a mighty way.

Chapter 6
The Anonymous Evangelist

Chapter Summary

This chapter focuses on the unnamed evangelist, who was seen by Jesus and brought back to the fullness of life, and whose witness led a whole community to experience Jesus as well.

Reflection / Discussion Questions

1. What spin does the author put on the life of the woman of Samaria before she met Jesus? How is that different from the traditional perception of her?

2. Why do you think the woman went to the well during a time of day when few others would be there?

3. Have you ever felt the need to hide? Describe the feelings associated with hiding. As with Adam and Eve in the garden, running sometimes seems to come almost naturally. What brought you out of hiding?

4. Jesus broke many cultural boundaries in speaking to this woman. What types of cultural boundaries do you have to face?

5. Can you describe what Jesus' face might have looked like as he told this woman what had been said about her, both in and out of her presence, for years?

6. Describe what you think went through the woman's mind when she said, "I know that Messiah is coming," and Jesus replied to her, *"I am he"* (John 4:25-26).

7. The author suggested that this Samaritan woman was "a seeker." What is your definition of a *seeker*?

8. What might have caused the other people in this woman's community to "come and see"?

9. Recall and reflect on an unlikely witness who unexpectedly boosted you along in your journey of faith. How can you honor her today?

10. Isaiah 49:14-16 tells us that the Lord inscribes us on the palm of his hand, that although all may forget us, God keeps a record that is eternal (Isaiah 49:16). How do you think this revelation was significant to the Anonymous Evangelist, and how might it be significant for you?

11. How have your reading, reflection, and discussion of chapter 6 helped or challenged you? What other important points or questions from this chapter would you like to explore?

Prayer Focus

Sometimes we let sin that we have committed in the past keep us hiding, and we are reluctant to broach the subject with God. Talk with God. Let God come and tell you what he sees, and then allow God to fill the void in your life.

If there is a sin that is too difficult to face alone, pray for a trustworthy friend to confess to. Ask Jesus to be present with you and to bring water to the dry places.

Thank you, Lord, that you come to us, even when we think we should be in hiding. Nothing is beyond your redemption!

Chapter 7
Mary Magdalene:
When Love Is Greater Than Faith

Chapter Summary

This chapter focuses on Mary Magdalene, who has been misunderstood for ages, was found by Jesus and spent the rest of her life in devotion to him.

Reflection / Discussion Questions

1. Why did Mary Magdalene go to the tomb early, "while it was still dark" (John 20:1)?

2. What was Mary expecting to find at the tomb? What did she find instead?

3. What does the author tell us about the significance of lightness and darkness in John's Gospel?

4. How do you explain a "hopeless case" like Mary's?

5. What was the difference in Mary's life after her encounter with Jesus?

6. According to the author, how did the other people in Mary's community most likely respond to her?

7. What impact can a story like Mary's have upon a group of believers?

8. Does one need an intense encounter with the Lord, or a major deliverance experience, to be considered a true follower of Christ? Why or why not?

9. Recall and share a time in your life when the darkness was thick, and tell how you managed to walk through it.

10. Does God still work today as he did in Mary's life? Explain. Recall and reflect upon a story of God's transforming love, and share it with someone near you today.

11. How have your reading, reflection, and discussion of chapter 7 helped or challenged you? What other important points or questions from this chapter would you like to explore?

Prayer Focus

Are there any Marys in your life who are in particular need of a touch from the living God? Will you ask God how you can love those persons today?

Controversy seemed to surround Mary throughout her life, and it continues even today. Mary may have needed a reminder from time to time of who she was. Looking at Jesus, her Redeemer, would have helped tremendously at such times. Would you sit with Jesus and ask him who he sees you to be? He may give you a picture or a word or a name or a feeling. He might even give you a song. If you do not get a response right away, keep asking. He will answer.

Dear God, though we may not have experienced the darkness of Mary Magdalene, give us the love and devotion that carried her through, that we too might testify far and wide to your love and power.

Chapter 8
Mary, the Mother of Mark

Chapter Summary

This chapter focuses on Mary, the Mother of Mark, a woman of courage who opened her home and her resources, knowing that it could mean losing everything, including her life.

Reflection / Discussion Questions

1. What were the dangers of following Jesus openly in the days of the early Christian church?

2. What do we know of Mary, the mother of Mark, and what can we infer about her based on a reading of Acts 12:6-17?

3. What could have made Mary so intent on keeping the Christian fellowship going?

4. What example does Mary's tenacity in following the Lord set for the church today?

5. What is your definition of *femininity*? How does Mary fit into that definition of femininity?

6. How was Mary an example of what ministry can look like at home? What principles from Mary's life could be applied in workplaces outside of the home?

7. Recall and share the story of a courageous woman in

your life, someone who has helped make it possible for you to grow in faith.

8. What challenges do today's followers of Christ face when it comes to being faithful?

9. What resources have you been gifted with that might help bring other followers of Christ deeper into the place of communion with God and with one another? (If it is hard to find an answer just now, discuss with a friend.)

10. In what places or circumstances are you called to be courageous?

11. How have your reading, reflection, and discussion of chapter 8 helped or challenged you? What other important points or questions from this chapter would you like to explore?

Prayer Focus

After determining the areas in which you need to be courageous, brainstorm with another person the steps that you can take to grow in your faith. These steps will look different for different people, as all of us are created differently.

What does courage look like for you? After identifying steps you can take toward growth, take action on at least one of those steps this week.

Ask the Lord, as often as you dare, to do what he needs to do in order to make you a fearless follower of him, courageous no matter the circumstances.

Thank you, Lord, that with you, nothing is impossible. With you, we are able to stand in the face of all circumstances, knowing that we are yours, and that nothing can change that.

Chapter 9
Dorcas: Worth a Miracle

Chapter Summary

This chapter focuses on Dorcas, a woman who was so imperative to the life of the community that an outpouring following her death preceded the miracle of her new life.

Reflection / Discussion Questions

1. What was significant about Dorcas's name?

2. Why might Luke, the author of Acts, have felt that Dorcas's story needed to be included in the Gospel?

3. What do we know about the life of Dorcas?

4. Why did the people of Joppa feel that Dorcas was "worth a miracle"?

5. To what modern woman might you compare Dorcas? How are the two women different? How are they similar?

6. Is the church today responsible for caring for persons who are orphaned and widowed? Why or why not? What might that sort of care look like in our world today?

7. Who is someone in your life you feel would be "worth a miracle," and for what reasons?

8. Take a moment and read John 3:16. How might what is described there be considered a miracle? What does it mean to you personally?

9. Healing comes in many forms, and in this case, Jesus brought Dorcas back to life from the dead. Can you recall and share a story of someone who has come alive again because of Jesus Christ?

10. In what ways does the story of Dorcas challenge you? How might you respond to that challenge?

11. How have your reading, reflection, and discussion of chapter 9 helped or challenged you? What other important points or questions from this chapter would you like to explore?

Prayer Focus

Reflect on Dorcas and the type of life she led, including her many acts of charity. Ask God to use you and your gifts to serve others, in Jesus' name.

Talk with someone about how to look with the eyes of the Lord and see all people as worthy of a miracle, as worthy of the saving grace of Jesus Christ.

Thank you, Lord, that you sent Jesus Christ, the miracle of all miracles, that with a touch from him, we too could be brought back to life.

Chapter 10
Lydia, the Businesswoman

Chapter Summary

This chapter focuses on Lydia, a businesswoman whose time of prayer down by the river led her to Christ, and who became a strong leader in the early Christian church.

Reflection / Discussion Questions

1. How was Jesus' attitude toward women different from the attitude within the culture of his time?

2. What did Paul's attitude toward women look like in his life? in his writings?

3. Where was Lydia located, and what was the character of the city in which she lived?

4. What do we know about Lydia's life and her trade?

5. What were the strengths of Lydia's character?

6. What effect did Lydia's listening have on her life and on the lives of others in her community?

7. What might have helped prepare Lydia for what Paul had to share down at the river's edge?

8. Why might the message of Jesus Christ have been particularly good news for Lydia?

9. How might Lydia have used her business activities to share the gospel? What does the combination of business and Christianity look like to you? How can they work together?

10. Lydia showed tremendous fortitude in various aspects of her life. Recall and share a story of a woman who has shown such fortitude and who has had an impact upon your life.

11. How have your reading, reflection, and discussion of chapter 10 helped or challenged you? What other important points or questions from this chapter would you like to explore?

Prayer Focus

One of Lydia's points along her journey of becoming a follower of Jesus Christ was meeting with others to pray along the river. Take some time to make some sort of tangible record of your faith journey thus far. What does your time "by the river" look like? If you don't have such a time, would you be willing to find a few others with whom to sit "by the river" and seek the Lord?

Thank you, Lord, that business and faith do not have to be mutually exclusive. Teach me to listen as Lydia did, that I might lead others to you as well.

Chapter 11
Mary in Life and Legend

Chapter Summary

This chapter focuses on Mary, the mother of Jesus, who accepted her calling with a song of praise, and whose unique position in history has led to dramatic interpretations of her character and her life.

Reflection / Discussion Questions

1. How did God prepare the people for the virgin birth?

2. God could have made Jesus Christ from the dust, as he did Adam. What might have been the significance of sending Jesus to be born through Mary?

3. What do we know about Mary's background?

4. What was Mary's response to the angelic visitation?

5. What was Mary's response after the crucifixion of Jesus?

6. What did Mary's part in the early church look like?

7. Why do you believe some people may find it comforting to pray through Mary to God, rather than approaching God firsthand?

8. The author says that often, "We are so absorbed with the immediate that we are hardly open to the transcendent." How can we develop that quality of being open to the transcendent in the midst of our often hectic lives?

9. Amid the Scripture, dogmas, and legends of Mary, what is the single most important thing to remember about her?

10. Mary's mission was perfect for her. What is the awesome mission created for you and only you? (If you do not know, sit for a while in prayer with God, and ask.)

11. How have your reading, reflection, and discussion of chapter 11 helped or challenged you? What other important points or questions from this chapter would you like to explore?

Prayer Focus

If possible, talk to someone who is Catholic, and listen to his or her perspective on praying to Mary. Though not all denominations or Christian faith traditions agree on every point, there is much we can learn from one another.

When Mary was visited by the angel and told her mission, she was moved to offer a song of praise. Write a song of praise, or a poem, or some other sort of praise to the Lord for who God is to you.

Thank you, Lord, that you give us a frame, and a gift to go with that frame, that will allow us, in your strength, to be faithful to our calling.

Chapter 12
Why Mary?

Chapter Summary

This chapter continues the focus on Mary, the mother of Jesus, who was chosen by God to walk a joyous and painful journey, and who was faithful to the end.

Reflection / Discussion Questions

1. Mary was visited by an angel sent from God, who carried the message of Mary's mission. What do we know of what followed in Mary's story that may have helped her process this awesome prophecy?

2. What sorts of thoughts do you believe went through Mary's mind on her way to see Elizabeth?

3. Throughout Scripture, many people who were called by God were terrified by the magnitude of their callings. Some even ran away to hide. Mary responded to her calling in a different manner. How do you think she might have been prepared for the angelic visitation?

4. Describe Mary's situation and circumstances at the time of Jesus' birth.

5. What were some of the challenges Mary faced during Jesus' upbringing?

6. What were some of the later challenges in Jesus' life that Mary had to face?

7. Recall and share something about a woman you know who was faithful to the task of motherhood. What made this woman special?

8. What are the challenges you face as you walk along on your faith journey, or as you seek to respond to God's call in your life?

9. The author notes that "God chose well" with Mary. What portion of her life and journey would make you most inclined to agree?

10. How has God chosen well with you?

11. How have your reading, reflection, and discussion of chapter 12 helped or challenged you? What other important points or questions from this chapter would you like to explore?

Prayer Focus

If you are a mother—biologically or spiritually—reflect on your experience of watching the triumphs and sorrows of your children. You might also ask a mother near you to recall and share her experiences. Reflect on some of the emotions and thoughts Mary may have had during the thirty-three years she spent on earth with Jesus.

Reflect on what has made the deepest impact upon you as you have read and discussed this book. Ask the Lord to teach you more about those things in the days ahead.

Dear God, thank you that you have crafted each of us with gifts that fit magnificently into your plan. Please continue to grant us the Holy Spirit to guide us in the use of those gifts and to guide us deeper into your heart.

Notes

1. Elizabeth: A Friend in Need

1. William Barclay, *The Gospel of Luke* (Philadelphia: The Westminster Press, 1956), 4.

3. Martha, the Disciplined

1. Elisabeth Moltmann-Wendel, *The Women Around Jesus* (New York: Crossroad, 1997), 20.

6. The Anonymous Evangelist

1. Henry Sloane Coffin, *Joy in Believing* (New York: Charles Scribner's Sons, 1956), 29.

9. Dorcas: Worth a Miracle

1. Walter F. Adeney, *Women of the New Testament* (London: Service & Paton, 1899), 209.
2. *The Interpreter's Bible,* volume 9 (Nashville: Abingdon Press, 1954), 129.

10. Lydia, the Businesswoman

1. Jimmy Carter, "Back to Fundamentals," *Christian Century,* September 20, 2005, 33.

2. William Barclay, *The Acts of the Apostles* (Philadelphia: The Westminster Press, 1955), 133.

11. Mary in Life and Legend

1. Ruth Bordin, *Frances Willard* (Chapel Hill: University of North Carolina Press, 1986), 4.

2. From the Nicene Creed, *The United Methodist Hymnal* (Nashville: The United Methodist Publishing House, 1989), 880.

3. Phyllis McGinley, *Saint Watching* (New York: Viking Press, 1969), 189.

CPSIA information can be obtained at www.ICGtesting.com
Printed in the USA
LVOW08s0619150114

369418LV00005B/251/P